## Teach & Test

W9-CEP-618

# Reading Grade 3

## Table of Contents

# How to Use This Book

1. This book can be used in a home or classroom setting. Read through each unit before working with the student(s). Familiarize yourself with the vocabulary and the skills that are introduced at the top of each unit activity page. Use this information as a guide to help instruct the student(s).

2. Choose a quiet place with little or no interruptions (including the telephone). Talk with the student(s) about the purpose of this book and how you will be working as a team to prepare for standardized tests.

3. As an option, copy the unit test and give it as a pretest to identify weak areas.

4. Upon the completion of each unit, you will find a unit test. Discuss the Helping Hand strategy for test taking featured on the test. Use the example on each test as a chance to show the student(s) how to work through a problem and completely fill in the answer circle. Encourage the student(s) to work independently when possible, but this is a learning time, and questions should be welcomed. A time limit is given for each test. Instruct the student(s) to use the time allowed efficiently, looking back over the answers if possible. Tell him to continue until he sees the stop sign.

5. Record the score on the record sheet on page 4. If a student has difficulty with any questions, use the cross-reference guide on the inside back cover to identify the skills that need to be reviewed.

## Introduction

Now this makes sense—teaching students the skills and strategies that are expected of them before they are tested!

Many students, parents, and teachers are concerned that standardized test scores do not adequately reflect a child's capabilities. This may be due to one or more of the factors italicized below. The purpose of this book is to reduce the negative impact of these, or similar factors, on a student's standardized test scores. The goal is to target those factors and alter their effects as described.

1. *The student has been taught the tested skills but has forgotten them.* This book is divided into units that are organized similarly to third grade textbooks. Instructions for the skill itself are found at the top of each unit activity page, ensuring that the student has been exposed to each key component. The exercises include drill/practice and creative learning activities. Additional activity suggestions can be found in a star burst within the units. These activities require the student to apply the skills that they are practicing.

2. *The student has mastered the skills but has never seen them presented in a test-type format.* Ideally, the skills a student learns at school will be used as part of problem solving in the outside world. For this reason, the skills in this book, and in most classrooms, are not practiced in a test-type format. At the end of each unit in this book, the skills are specifically matched with test questions. In this way, the book serves as a type of "bridge" between the skills that the student(s) has mastered and the standardized test format.

3. *The student is inexperienced with the answer sheet format.* Depending on the standardized test that your school district uses, students are expected to use a fill-in-the-bubble name grid and score sheet. To familiarize students with this process, a name grid and score sheet are included for the review tests found at the midway point and again at the end of the book.

4. *The student may feel the anxiety of a new and unfamiliar situation.* While testing, students will notice changes in their daily routine: their classroom door will be closed with a "Testing" sign on it, they will be asked not to use the restroom, their desks may be separated, their teacher may read from a script and refuse to repeat herself, etc. To help relieve the stress caused by these changes, treat each unit test in this book as it would be treated at school by following the procedures listed below.

## Stage a Test

You will find review tests midway through the book and again at the end of the book. When you reach these points, "stage a test" by creating a real test-taking environment. The procedures listed below coincide with many standardized test directions. The purpose is to alleviate stress, rather than contribute to it, so make this a serious, but calm event and the student(s) will benefit.

1. Prepare! Have the student(s) sharpen two pencils, lay out scratch paper, and use the restroom.

2. Choose a room with a door that can be closed. Ask a student to put a sign on the door that reads "Testing" and explain that no talking will be permitted after the sign is hung.

3. Direct the student(s) to turn to a specific page but not to begin until the instructions are completely given.

4. Read the instructions at the top of the page and work through the example together. Discuss the Helping Hand strategy that is featured at the top of the page. Have the student(s) neatly and completely fill in the bubble for the example. This is the child's last chance to ask for help!

5. Instruct the student(s) to continue working until the stop sign is reached. If a student needs help reading, you may read each question only once.

# Helping Hand Test Strategies

The first page of each test features a specific test-taking strategy that will be helpful in working through most standardized tests. These strategies are introduced and spotlighted one at a time so that they will be learned and remembered internally. Each will serve as a valuable test-taking tool, so discuss them thoroughly.

The strategies include:

- If you are unsure, try each answer in the blank.
- When working with a dictionary, table of contents, or index, use your finger to keep your place.
- Read all of the answer choices before you decide.
- Watch for key words in the story that give you clues.
- Reread the paragraphs if you cannot remember an answer.
- More than one answer may seem correct! Be sure to compare the choices.
- Use your time wisely. If something seems too tough, skip it and come back later.
- Take time to review your answers.

# Constructed-Response Questions

You will find the final question(s) of the tests are written in a different format called constructed response. This means that students are not provided with answer choices, but are instead asked to construct their own answers. The objective of such an "open-ended" type of question is to provide students with a chance to creatively develop reasonable answers. It also provides an insight to a student's reasoning and thinking skills. As this format is becoming more accepted and encouraged by standardized test developers, students will be "ahead of the game" by practicing such responses now.

# Evaluating the Tests

Two types of questions are included in each test. The unit tests and the midway review test each consist of 20 multiple-choice questions, and the final review test consists of 25 multiple-choice questions. All tests include a constructed-response question which requires the student(s) to construct and sometimes support an answer. Use the following procedures to evaluate a student's performance on each test.

1. Use the answer key found on pages 126–128 to correct the tests. Be sure the student(s) neatly and completely filled in the answer circles.

2. Record the scores on the record sheet found on page 4. If the student(s) incorrectly answered any questions, use the cross-reference guide found on the inside back cover to help identify the skills the student(s) needs to review. Each test question references the corresponding activity page.

3. Scoring the constructed-response questions is somewhat subjective. Discuss these questions with the student(s). Sometimes it is easier for the student(s) to explain the answer verbally. Help the student to record his or her thoughts as a written answer. If the student(s) has difficulty formulating a response, refer back to the activity pages using the cross-reference guide. Also review the star burst activity found in the unit which also requires the student(s) to formulate an answer.

4. Discuss the test with the student(s). What strategies were used to answer the questions? Were some questions more difficult than others? Was there enough time? What strategies did the student(s) use while taking the test?

# Record Sheet

Record a student's score for each test by drawing a star or placing a sticker below each item number that was correct. Leave the incorrect boxes empty as this will allow you to visually see any weak spots. Review and practice those missed skills, then retest only the necessary items.

| Unit 1 | 1 | 2 | 3 | 4 | 5 | 6 | 7 | 8 | 9 | 10 | 11 | 12 | 13 | 14 | 15 | 16 | 17 | 18 | 19 | 20 |
|---|---|---|---|---|---|---|---|---|---|---|---|---|---|---|---|---|---|---|---|---|
|  |  |  |  |  |  |  |  |  |  |  |  |  |  |  |  |  |  |  |  |  |

| Unit 2 | 1 | 2 | 3 | 4 | 5 | 6 | 7 | 8 | 9 | 10 | 11 | 12 | 13 | 14 | 15 | 16 | 17 | 18 | 19 | 20 |
|---|---|---|---|---|---|---|---|---|---|---|---|---|---|---|---|---|---|---|---|---|
|  |  |  |  |  |  |  |  |  |  |  |  |  |  |  |  |  |  |  |  |  |  |

| Unit 3 | 1 | 2 | 3 | 4 | 5 | 6 | 7 | 8 | 9 | 10 | 11 | 12 | 13 | 14 | 15 | 16 | 17 | 18 | 19 | 20 |
|---|---|---|---|---|---|---|---|---|---|---|---|---|---|---|---|---|---|---|---|---|
|  |  |  |  |  |  |  |  |  |  |  |  |  |  |  |  |  |  |  |  |  |  |

| Unit 4 | 1 | 2 | 3 | 4 | 5 | 6 | 7 | 8 | 9 | 10 | 11 | 12 | 13 | 14 | 15 | 16 | 17 | 18 | 19 | 20 |
|---|---|---|---|---|---|---|---|---|---|---|---|---|---|---|---|---|---|---|---|---|
|  |  |  |  |  |  |  |  |  |  |  |  |  |  |  |  |  |  |  |  |  |  |

| Midway Review Test | 1 | 2 | 3 | 4 | 5 | 6 | 7 | 8 | 9 | 10 | 11 | 12 | 13 | 14 | 15 | 16 | 17 | 18 | 19 | 20 |
|---|---|---|---|---|---|---|---|---|---|---|---|---|---|---|---|---|---|---|---|---|---|
|  |  |  |  |  |  |  |  |  |  |  |  |  |  |  |  |  |  |  |  |  |  |  |

| Unit 5 | 1 | 2 | 3 | 4 | 5 | 6 | 7 | 8 | 9 | 10 | 11 | 12 | 13 | 14 | 15 | 16 | 17 | 18 | 19 | 20 |
|---|---|---|---|---|---|---|---|---|---|---|---|---|---|---|---|---|---|---|---|---|
|  |  |  |  |  |  |  |  |  |  |  |  |  |  |  |  |  |  |  |  |  |  |

| Unit 6 | 1 | 2 | 3 | 4 | 5 | 6 | 7 | 8 | 9 | 10 | 11 | 12 | 13 | 14 | 15 | 16 | 17 | 18 | 19 | 20 |
|---|---|---|---|---|---|---|---|---|---|---|---|---|---|---|---|---|---|---|---|---|
|  |  |  |  |  |  |  |  |  |  |  |  |  |  |  |  |  |  |  |  |  |  |

| Unit 7 | 1 | 2 | 3 | 4 | 5 | 6 | 7 | 8 | 9 | 10 | 11 | 12 | 13 | 14 | 15 | 16 | 17 | 18 | 19 | 20 |
|---|---|---|---|---|---|---|---|---|---|---|---|---|---|---|---|---|---|---|---|---|
|  |  |  |  |  |  |  |  |  |  |  |  |  |  |  |  |  |  |  |  |  |  |

| Unit 8 | 1 | 2 | 3 | 4 | 5 | 6 | 7 | 8 | 9 | 10 | 11 | 12 | 13 | 14 | 15 | 16 | 17 | 18 | 19 | 20 |
|---|---|---|---|---|---|---|---|---|---|---|---|---|---|---|---|---|---|---|---|---|
|  |  |  |  |  |  |  |  |  |  |  |  |  |  |  |  |  |  |  |  |  |  |

| Final Review Test | 1 | 2 | 3 | 4 | 5 | 6 | 7 | 8 | 9 | 10 | 11 | 12 | 13 | 14 | 15 | 16 | 17 | 18 | 19 | 20 |
|---|---|---|---|---|---|---|---|---|---|---|---|---|---|---|---|---|---|---|---|---|---|
|  |  |  |  |  |  |  |  |  |  |  |  |  |  |  |  |  |  |  |  |  |  |  |

| 21 | 22 | 23 | 24 | 25 |
|---|---|---|---|---|
|  |  |  |  |  |

Name

**Synonyms** are words that have almost the same meaning.

Examples:
| complete | bunch | meet |
| finish | group | join |

Find a synonym on the racetrack for each word below. Write the number next to the word. Be sure to work in order to move the race cars forward. Circle the car whose path is finished first and becomes the winner of the Great Word Race!

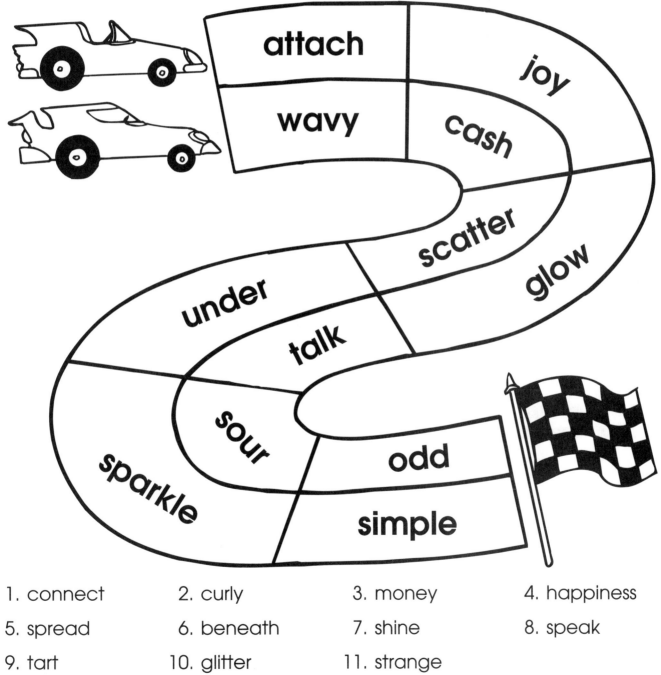

attach

wavy

joy

cash

scatter

glow

under

talk

sour

sparkle

odd

simple

1. connect
2. curly
3. money
4. happiness
5. spread
6. beneath
7. shine
8. speak
9. tart
10. glitter
11. strange

## Using synonyms

If you are unsure of the correct synonym, try using each word in its place.

Complete the puzzle by matching the underlined word with its synonym. Use the words in the Word Bank to help you.

### Across

3. Do you <u>recall</u> the phone number?

6. I was so <u>famished</u> that I ate two plates of spaghetti.

7. There was a huge <u>mob</u> of fans outside the concert.

9. Your birthday party was <u>superb</u>!

### Down

1. On Monday, a <u>famous</u> artist will visit our school.

2. My dog is so <u>intelligent</u> that he learned three new tricks in one day.

4. My aunt <u>grasped</u> the railing as she came down the stairs.

5. Jack's puppy likes to <u>gnaw</u> on his bone.

8. My mom took me to our <u>physician</u> when I got sick.

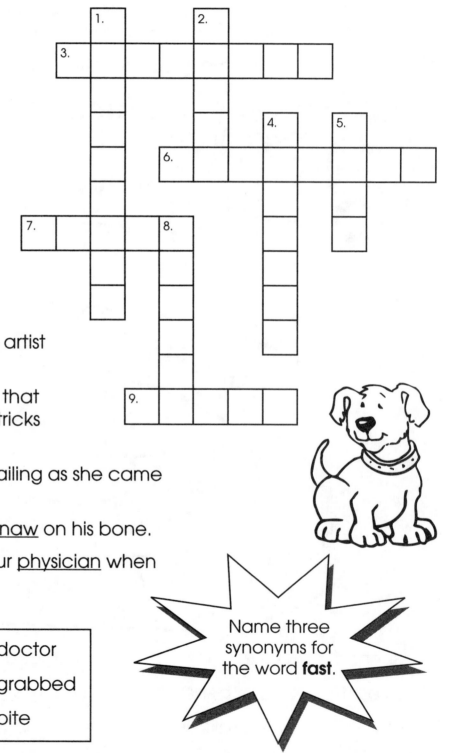

Name three synonyms for the word **fast**.

| remember | smart | doctor |
| --- | --- | --- |
| well-known | great | grabbed |
| starving | crowd | bite |

Name

**Antonyms** are words with opposite meanings.

Examples:  raise        asleep        leave
              lower        awake        arrive

Read each word below. Find its antonym in the Word Bank and write it in the boxes. To find the answer to the riddle, read the letters in the bold boxes going down.

**What travels all around the world, yet always stays in the corner!**

A ___ ___ ___ ___ ___ ___        ___ ___ ___ ___ ___!

| adult | brave | remember | silent | cheap | filthy |
| whole | begin | dangerous | stretch | playful | catch |

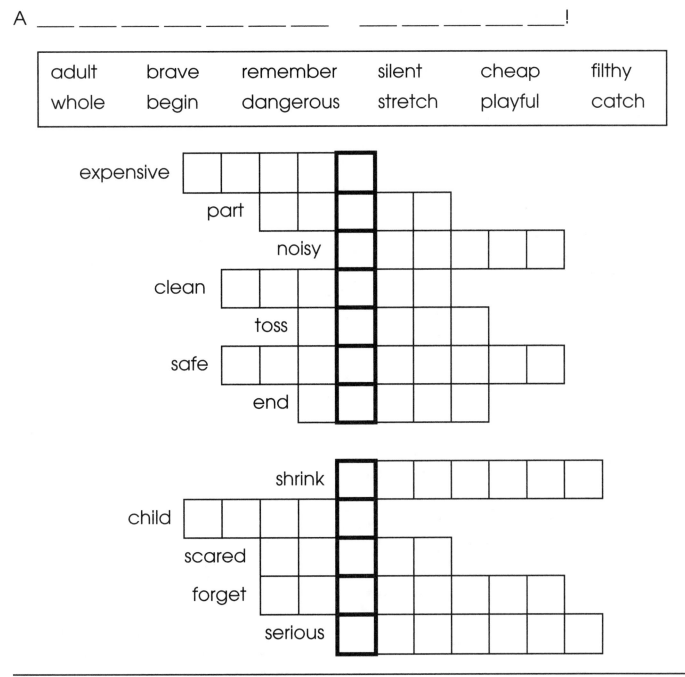

expensive

part

noisy

clean

toss

safe

end

shrink

child

scared

forget

serious

Name

Find the antonym for each underlined word in the Word Bank. Write its letter on the basket of each balloon.

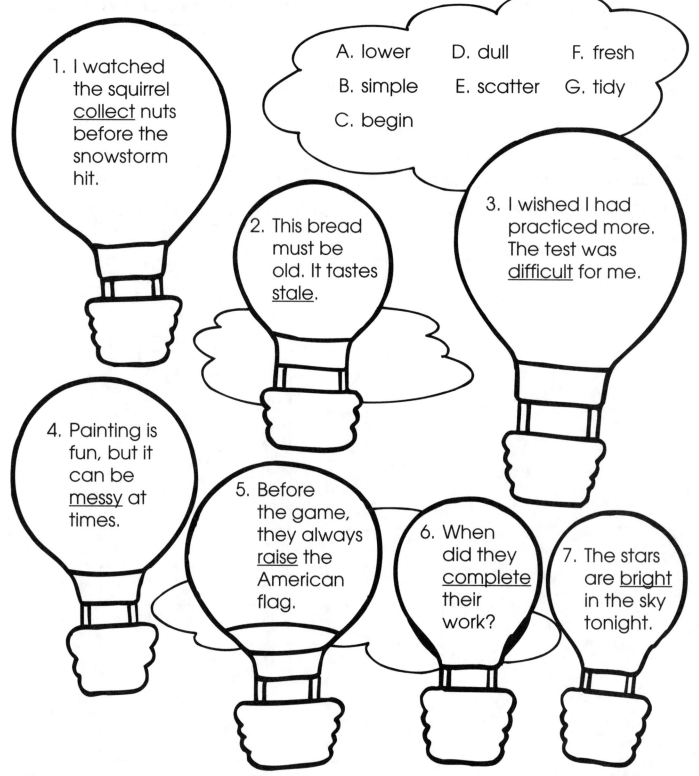

A. lower  D. dull  F. fresh

B. simple  E. scatter  G. tidy

C. begin

1. I watched the squirrel collect nuts before the snowstorm hit.

2. This bread must be old. It tastes stale.

3. I wished I had practiced more. The test was difficult for me.

4. Painting is fun, but it can be messy at times.

5. Before the game, they always raise the American flag.

6. When did they complete their work?

7. The stars are bright in the sky tonight.

Name _____

## Multiple meaning words

Many of the words we use look and sound the same, but have different meanings.
We know which meaning makes sense by reading the sentence.

Write the word from the Word Bank that makes sense in both sentences.

| tire | break | mean | straw | land | glasses | book | free |
|------|-------|------|-------|------|---------|------|------|

1. Be careful not to _____ Mom's favorite vase.

   Should we take a _____ from practice to eat lunch?

2. Mom is going to _____ an appointment for Monday.

   Have you read the new _____ by J. K. Rowling?

3. What do you _____ by that?

   The dog that lives next door is _____, so let's stay away.

4. My cat is so old that chasing a mouse will _____ her out.

   We had a flat _____ when we were driving to Florida.

5. The plane is due to _____ at 6:00 tonight.

   The large pieces of _____ on Earth are called continents.

6. The zookeeper lifted the door to _____ the bird.

   I can't believe we read enough books to earn _____ pizza!

7. After you finish, set your lemonade _____ on the counter.

   I am going to get new _____ to help me see the board.

8. The farmer keeps _____ in the barn during the winter.

   Can you hand me a _____ for my milk shake?

Name

## Using multiple meaning words

Unit 1

A dictionary will help you discover the multiple meanings of a word.

The words below are multiple meaning words. Write two sentences for each word that use different meanings.

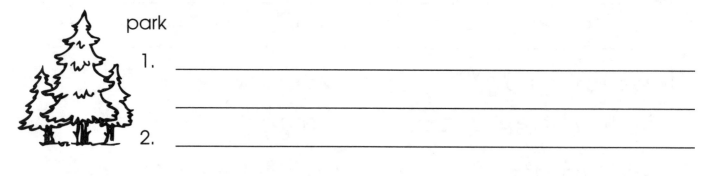

park

1. _____

_____

2. _____

_____

hand

1. _____

_____

2. _____

_____

bat

1. _____

_____

2. _____

_____

Name

## Using context clues

Have you ever come to a word that you can sound out, but you do not know what it means? One way to find its meaning is to use all of the other words to figure out what would make sense. This is called using **context clues**. Using the rest of the sentence will give you clues about the unknown word's meaning.

This picture shows some parts of a volcano. Use the context clues from each sentence to label the picture using the underlined words.

1. Some people think volcanoes start at the <u>core</u> of the earth. This is not true.

2. Inside the <u>magma chamber</u>, hot liquid is pushing up.

3. The <u>rock plug</u> finally blows into the air, making an opening at the top of the volcano.

4. Clouds of <u>gas</u> rise into the air.

5. Hot <u>lava</u> flows down the sides of the volcano.

6. At last nothing more comes through the <u>vent</u>.

7. <u>Tuff</u> will form around the volcano as the ashes cool.

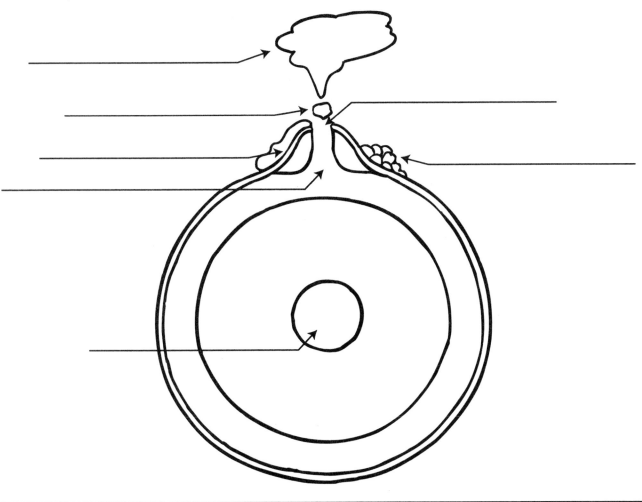

Name

# Using context clues

Sometimes the context clues along with your own ideas will help you make a good guess at a word's meaning,

Use the context clues to make the best choice for each word's meaning.

1. Most small children are <u>forbidden</u> to cross the street without an adult.

   ○ helped        ○ told not to        ○ forced

2. Tracy buttoned her <u>cardigan</u> to keep warm at the game.

   ○ sweater        ○ pajamas        ○ boots

3. The autumn morning <u>dew</u> left the playground damp.

   ○ clumps of snow        ○ pieces of ice        ○ drops of water

4. Dad likes to <u>relax</u> on the sofa after he takes us swimming.

   ○ jump        ○ rest        ○ sleep

5. Our team must be <u>united</u> if we want to win the championship.

   ○ working together    ○ awake        ○ dressed up

6. I remember that type of butterfly by its <u>distinct</u> markings.

   ○ yellow        ○ special        ○ dirty

7. The balloon <u>burst</u> as it brushed against the brick wall.

   ○ flew higher        ○ got away        ○ popped

8. Some Native Americans made their <u>dwellings</u> in the rocks.

   ○ shoes        ○ blankets        ○ homes

9. The tarantula spider has tiny <u>bristles</u> on its legs that can prick its enemy.

   ○ spots        ○ sharp hairs        ○ teeth

Name

Read or listen to the directions. Fill in the circle beside the best answer.

❑ Example:

Mark the word that has two meanings.

(A) you    (B) friend

(C) ant    (D) top

Answer: D because top can mean:
    1. a toy that spins or
    2. the highest part of something.

If you are unsure, try each answer in the blank.

Now try these. You have 20 minutes. Continue until you see ⬡STOP.

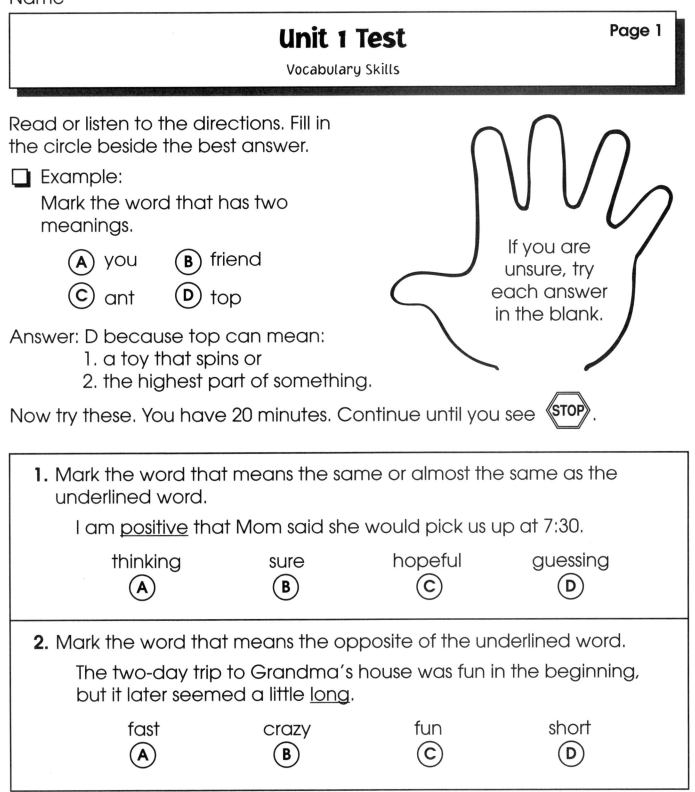

---

1. Mark the word that means the same or almost the same as the underlined word.

    I am <u>positive</u> that Mom said she would pick us up at 7:30.

    thinking       sure       hopeful       guessing
    (A)         (B)        (C)        (D)

---

2. Mark the word that means the opposite of the underlined word.

    The two-day trip to Grandma's house was fun in the beginning, but it later seemed a little <u>long</u>.

    fast       crazy       fun       short
    (A)        (B)       (C)       (D)

GO ON

**3.** Choose a word from the list that has different meanings, but makes sense in both sentences.

1. _____ of paint are falling off the old barn door.

2. Last, we added chocolate _____ to the recipe.

| lots | milk | chips | cake |
|------|------|-------|------|
| (A) | (B) | (C) | (D) |

Mark the word that makes sense in each sentence.

**4.** Did you _____ the package I sent you for your birthday?

| receive | send | clean | attend |
|---------|------|-------|--------|
| (A) | (B) | (C) | (D) |

**5.** I was a little _____ in mailing it. I hope it made it in time.

| funny | awkward | tardy | tight |
|-------|---------|-------|-------|
| (A) | (B) | (C) | (D) |

**6.** Mark the word that means almost the same as the underlined word.

amazing <u>strength</u>

| change | work | thoughts | power |
|--------|------|----------|-------|
| (A) | (B) | (C) | (D) |

**7.** Mark the word that means the opposite of **attached**.

| separate | joined | repaired | cracked |
|----------|--------|----------|---------|
| (A) | (B) | (C) | (D) |

GO ON

**8.** Mark the sentence in which the underlined word has the same meaning as the underlined word in the sentence below.

My cat's white fur looked <u>light</u> gray after playing in the fireplace.

(A) The lantern gave us <u>light</u> at night.

(B) She wore a <u>light</u> blue sweater.

(C) Remember to turn off the <u>light</u> when you leave.

(D) Only adults should <u>light</u> the candles.

**9.** Mark the word that means about the same as **precise**.

fruit
(A)

repeat
(B)

gift
(C)

exact
(D)

**10.** Use the context of the sentence to mark the picture of the <u>pelican</u>.

The <u>pelican</u> has a long bill for catching fish and webbed feet for swimming.

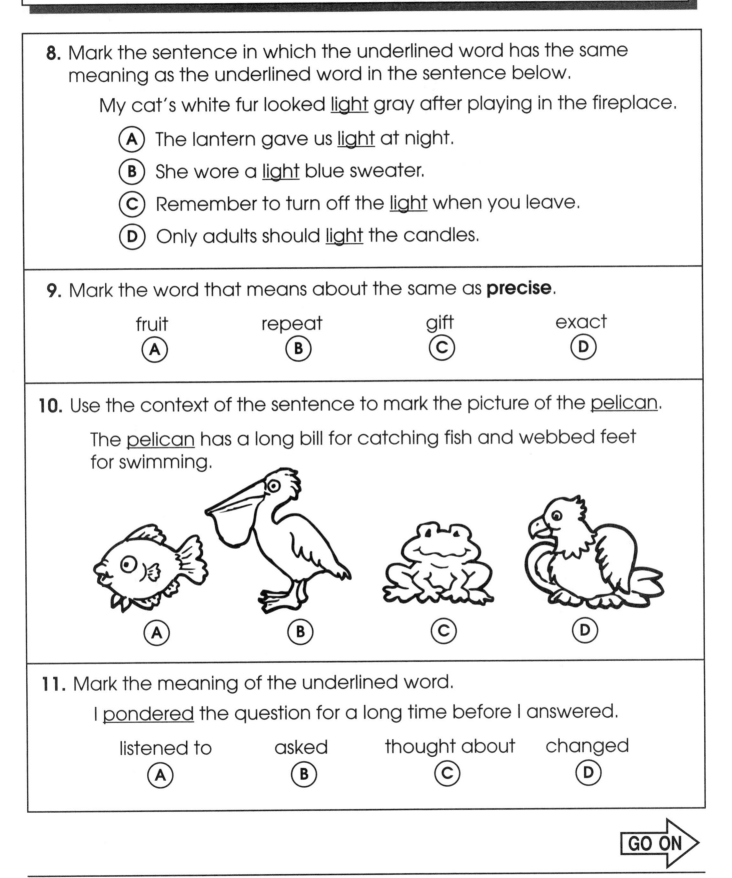

(A)     (B)     (C)     (D)

**11.** Mark the meaning of the underlined word.

I <u>pondered</u> the question for a long time before I answered.

listened to
(A)

asked
(B)

thought about
(C)

changed
(D)

GO ON

**12.** Mark the word that is the antonym of **wide**.

wavy
(A)

rare
(B)

wild
(C)

narrow
(D)

**13.** Which word has two meanings?

fit
(A)

sea
(B)

napkin
(C)

automobile
(D)

Choose the correct words to complete the sentence.

As the race cars _____ the turn the drivers will steer their cars
(14)

in another _____.
(15)

**14.** (A) length   (B) approach   |   **15.** (A) place   (B) signal

(C) increase   (D) toward   |   (C) direction   (D) hour

**16.** Identify the word that is a synonym for the underlined word.

a small <u>portion</u>

animal
(A)

space
(B)

mistake
(C)

part
(D)

**17.** Mark the word that means the opposite of the underlined word.

a <u>piece</u> of pie

plate
(A)

dessert
(B)

slice
(C)

whole
(D)

GO ON

**18.** Choose a word from the list that has different meanings but makes sense in both sentences.

    1. My puppy likes to stretch out on my _____.

    2. The _____ of snow covering the ground is beautiful.

| sheets | pour | blanket | covers |
|:---:|:---:|:---:|:---:|
| (A) | (B) | (C) | (D) |

**19.** Mark the sentence in which the underlined word has the same meaning as the underlined word in the sentence below.

We asked the kindergarten students to <u>point</u> to the letters they heard.

(A) The firefighter made a good <u>point</u> about not playing with fire.

(B) <u>Point</u> to the person who will be your science partner.

(C) The roof of the house comes to a big <u>point</u> over the garage.

(D) The ladybug sat on the <u>point</u> of the leaf.

**20.** Use the context of the sentence to find the meaning of the underlined word.

The street will <u>veer</u> to the left as you come toward Lucy's house.

| turn | start | come | end |
|:---:|:---:|:---:|:---:|
| (A) | (B) | (C) | (D) |

Think of a word that has two meanings. Write a sentence for each meaning and underline the word in each.

1. _____

2. _____

STOP

Name

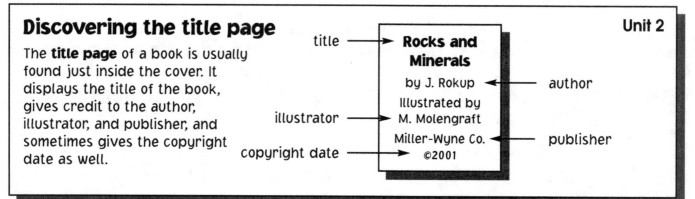

### Discovering the title page

The **title page** of a book is usually found just inside the cover. It displays the title of the book, gives credit to the author, illustrator, and publisher, and sometimes gives the copyright date as well.

title � **Rocks and Minerals**

by J. Rokup ◄─ author

illustrator ─► Illustrated by M. Molengraft

Miller-Wyne Co. ◄─ publisher

copyright date ─► ©2001

Unit 2

Design a title page for your favorite book below. Be sure to include the title, author, illustrator, publisher, and copyright date. Because these are all special names, they should also be capitalized.

## Using a table of contents

Most chapter books and longer informational books have a **table of contents** page after the title page. This helps you find parts of the book more quickly.

Your teacher has asked you to write a report about the human body. In the report, you must answer all of the questions listed below. It would take you a very long time to read the entire book, so you decide to use the table of contents to help you. Write the chapter and page number where you would begin looking to answer each question.

### Table of Contents

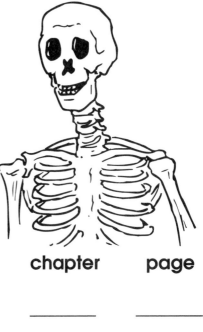

**chapter**     **page**

1.  How long does it take a piece of pizza to reach your stomach?   _____   _____

2.  How does your body know when something tastes sour?   _____   _____

3.  How many bones are in your skeleton?   _____   _____

4.  What color is your blood?   _____   _____

5.  How can you make yourself stronger?   _____   _____

6.  How fast do nerve impulses travel?   _____   _____

7.  Why do you have a belly button?   _____   _____

8.  Are there more bones in your hand or your foot?   _____   _____

9.  About how far can humans see?   _____   _____

10. How much of your body is made of water?   _____   _____

Name

## Using alphabetical order

Unit 2

To put words in **alphabetical order**, remember to look at the first letter of each word to find the letter that comes first in the alphabet. If they are the same, move on to the second letters. If they are the same, move on to the third letters, and so on.

Put each list of words in alphabetical order by numbering them **1–5**.

1.
_____ brag

_____ speak

_____ dreary

_____ united

_____ spool

2.
_____ brittle

_____ freeze

_____ beast

_____ yellow

_____ frown

3.
_____ weary

_____ trick

_____ salmon

_____ tragic

_____ quarrel

4.
_____ cabin

_____ spend

_____ shallow

_____ universe

_____ casement

5.
_____ grease

_____ gripe

_____ turkey

_____ evening

_____ grand

6.
_____ dive

_____ dungeon

_____ dump

_____ double

_____ dream

Write the names of your family members in alphabetical order.

Name

## Using an index

The **index** is found at the back of many informational books. It contains the main subjects that are covered in the book and their page numbers. The index lists the main headings, which are the main ideas in each subject area. Under the main headings, more specific details may also be listed in alphabetical order.

### Index

| Horses | 55, 57–59 |
|---|---|
| Houses | |
|     Cave | 34, 41–50 |
|     Native-American | 67 |
|     Modern | 14, 18, 21 |
| Humans | |
|     Babies | 89, 94–108 |
|     Children | 109–114 |
|     Adults | 115–121, 127 |
| Hunting | 51, 56 |
| Hurricanes | 12, 17 |

Use the index to find the answers. Then circle each answer.

1. Which page will not help you learn about babies?

    page 89            page 92            page 97

2. Which page will help you learn about hunting?

    page 12            page 56            page 115

3. Which type of house is not found in the book?

    cave            modern            shingle

4. Which page will not help you learn about houses?

    page 76            page 45            page 18

5. What will you learn about on page 111?

    adults            children            babies

6. What will you learn about on page 58?

    cave homes            hunting            horses

Name

## Using a dictionary

A **dictionary** is a book that does not tell a story, but instead lists nearly every word you can think of and its meaning. The word you look up in a dictionary is called the entry word, and its meaning is called the definition. If the word has more than one meaning, the definitions will be numbered.

Use the partial dictionary below to find the answers.

1. Which definition best fits the word <u>cry</u> as it is used in this sentence?

   The little girl <u>cried</u> out for her mother. Definition number _____

2. List other forms of the word <u>cute</u>. _____  _____

3. Which part of speech is the word <u>cream</u>? _____

4. Which definition best fits the word <u>crook</u> as it is used in this sentence?

   The <u>crook</u> stole the diamond from the museum. Definition number _____

5. Which part of speech is the word <u>dark</u>? _____

6. What is the definition of the word <u>dark</u>? _____

   _____

---

**cream** /krēm/ *noun, plural* **creams**. the yellowish-white part of milk. *Butter is made from cream.*

**crook** /krook/ *noun, plural* **crooks**. **1.** a bent part; curve. *I carry my umbrella in the crook of my arm.* **2.** a shepherd's staff with a hook at the top. **3.** a person who is not honest.

**cry** /krī/ *verb* **cried**, **crying**. **1.** to shed tears; weep. *The hungry baby cried.* **2.** to call out loudly; shout. *The people in the burning building were crying for help.*

**cute** /kūt/ *adjective* **cuter**, **cutest**. delightful or pretty. *This is the cutest puppy I have ever seen.*

**dark** /dark/ *adjective* having little or no light. *The night was dark because the clouds were covering the moon.*

**dash** /dash/ *verb* **dashed**, **dashing**. **1.** to move fast; rush. *We dashed to the waiting bus.* **2.** to destroy or ruin. *Spraining my ankle dashed my hopes of running in the race.* —*noun, plural* **dashes**. **1.** a fast movement or sudden rush. *When the rain began we made a dash for cover.* **2.** a small amount

Name

## Using a dictionary's entry words                          Unit 2

A dictionary gives definitions for nearly all words. To make it easier to find a particular
entry word, the entry words are listed in alphabetical order.

Oh no! This part of the dictionary is missing its entry words. Use the
sentences at the bottom to find the definition that makes sense for each
underlined word. Write the word in front of its definition. When you are
finished, the entry words should be in alphabetical order.

| | |
|---|---|
| | — a hooded robe |
| | — the part of milk used to make cheese |
| | — a type of bird |
| | — a fancy twist |
| | — a prickly brush |
| | — money |
| | — a leap by a horse |
| | — a type of fish |
| | — a greenish-blue color |

1. We laughed at the pig's <u>curlicue</u> tail.

2. The mysterious man wore a <u>cowl</u>.

3. My leg is scraped from rubbing against the <u>currant</u>.

4. The farmer collected <u>curd</u> from the milk pail.

5. In Mexico, the people pay for things with a different <u>currency</u>.

6. The ocean can be <u>cyan</u> in places.

7. The <u>curlew</u> flew right over our heads!

8. Mom fried <u>cusk</u> for dinner.

9. Did you see that horse <u>curvet</u>?

## Using a dictionary's guide words

**Guide words** are found in the top corners of each dictionary page. The word on the left is the very first word on that page. The word on the right is the very last word on that page. Guide words are helpful in "guiding" you to the word you need in a faster manner. You can flip through the dictionary looking only at guide words until you find the page where your word would fit.

What a mess! These entry words have gotten all scrambled up! Write them under the guide words where they belong.

| lamp | locket |
|------|--------|
| low | lobster |
| loud | learn |
| large | listen |
| lane | lot |
| lion | love |

| lamb | least |
|------|-------|
| 1. _____ | 2. _____ |
| 3. _____ | 4. _____ |

| licorice | loose |
|----------|-------|
| 5. _____ | 6. _____ |
| 7. _____ | 8. _____ |

| lost | lucky |
|------|-------|
| 9. _____ | 10. _____ |
| 11. _____ | 12. _____ |

Name

Read or listen to the directions. Fill in the circle beside the best answer.

☐ Example:

What is found at the back of informational books?

(A) title page

(B) index

(C) table of contents

(D) dictionary entry

When working with a dictionary, table of contents, or index, use your finger to keep your place.

Answer: B because an index is found at the back of informational books.

Now try these. You have 20 minutes.

Continue until you see ⬡STOP⬡.

Name the parts of the title page.

1. (A) title    (B) illustrator
   (C) author   (D) publisher

2. (A) title    (B) illustrator
   (C) author   (D) publisher

**Sailing**

by Karl French ← (1)

Illustrated by Gina Barron

THF and Co. ← (2)
©1998

3. Which comes first in alphabetical order?

comment       cozy          core          continue
(A)           (B)           (C)           (D)

GO ON →

**4.** Which of these materials would help you learn about the meaning of the word **evident**?

dictionary
Ⓐ

phone book
Ⓑ

index
Ⓒ

table of contents
Ⓓ

Use the table of contents to answer questions 5 and 6.

**Table of Contents**

| | | |
|---|---|---|
| Chapter 1 | Clouds | 3 |
| Chapter 2 | Wind | 13 |
| Chapter 3 | Rain and Hail | 22 |
| Chapter 4 | Snow and Sleet | 31 |
| Chapter 5 | Dangerous Weather | 40 |

**5.** Which chapter would help you learn about tornadoes?

Ⓐ 1    Ⓑ 2

Ⓒ 3    Ⓓ 5

**6.** What picture might you find if you turned to page 17?

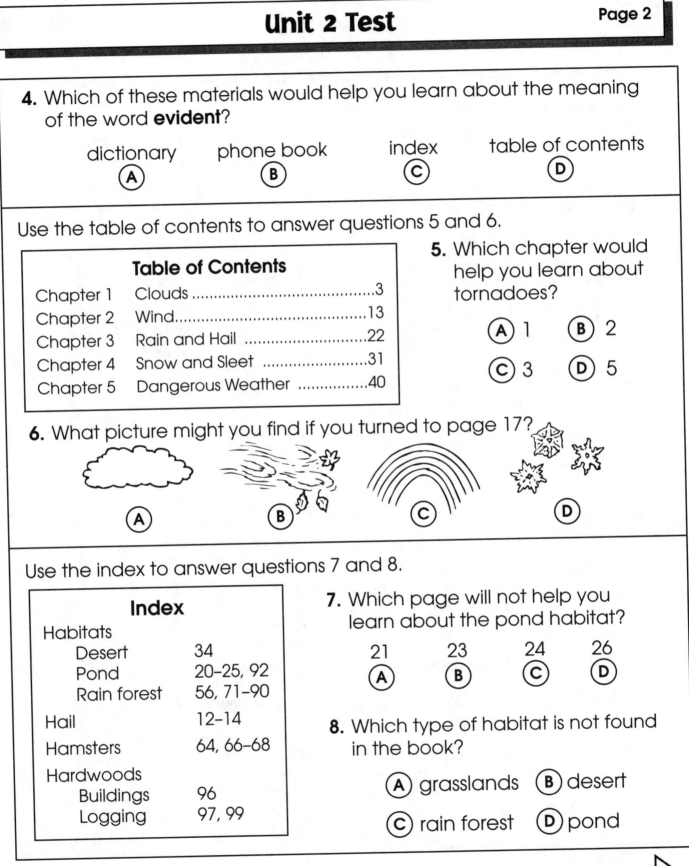

Ⓐ        Ⓑ        Ⓒ        Ⓓ

Use the index to answer questions 7 and 8.

**Index**

| Habitats | |
|---|---|
| Desert | 34 |
| Pond | 20–25, 92 |
| Rain forest | 56, 71–90 |
| Hail | 12–14 |
| Hamsters | 64, 66–68 |
| Hardwoods | |
| Buildings | 96 |
| Logging | 97, 99 |

**7.** Which page will not help you learn about the pond habitat?

21     23     24     26
Ⓐ     Ⓑ     Ⓒ     Ⓓ

**8.** Which type of habitat is not found in the book?

Ⓐ grasslands   Ⓑ desert

Ⓒ rain forest   Ⓓ pond

**GO ON**

Name

Use the dictionary below to answer questions 9–17.

**plan•et** /'plan-it/ *noun, plural* **planets**. one of nine large heavenly bodies that orbit the sun. *The planets in our solar system are Mercury, Venus, Earth, Mars, Jupiter, Saturn, Uranus, Neptune, and Pluto.*

**plate** /plāt/ *noun, plural* **plates**. a flat or shallow dish. *Food is served or eaten from plates.*

**plot** /plot/ *noun, plural* **plots**. 1. a secret plan. *The outlaws formed a plot to rob the stagecoach.* 2. the main story in a book, play, or movie. *That movie has an exciting plot.* 3. a small piece of ground. *We had our picnic on a grassy plot in the shade.*

**plum** /plum/ *noun, plural* **plums**. a soft, juicy fruit with a pit. *The tree has red plums.*

**plus** /plus/ *preposition*. with the addition of. *Two plus two is four.*

**pond** /pond/ *noun, plural* **ponds**. a small body of freshwater surrounded by land. *There are fish in the pond.*

**pool** /pool/ *noun, plural* **pools**. a tank of water to swim in, either indoors or outdoors. *The people next door to us have a pool.*

**pull** /pul/ *verb* **pulled, pulling**. to grab or hold something and move it forward or toward oneself. *Two horses pulled the wagon.*

**push** /push/ *verb* **pushed, pushing**. 1. to press on something in order to move it. *I pushed the cart through the market.* 2. to move forward with effort. *We had to push through the crowd.*

**put** /put/ *verb* **put, putting**. 1. to cause a thing or a person to be in a certain place, condition, or position; place; set. *Put the box on the table.* 2. to cause to undergo or experience. *You put them to a lot of trouble by being late.*

**9.** Which definition best fits the word <u>plot</u> as it is used in the sentence below?

We found the perfect <u>plot</u> to build our secret fort.

#1 Ⓐ    #2 Ⓑ    #3 Ⓒ

GO ON

Name _____

**10.** Which word does this picture best describe?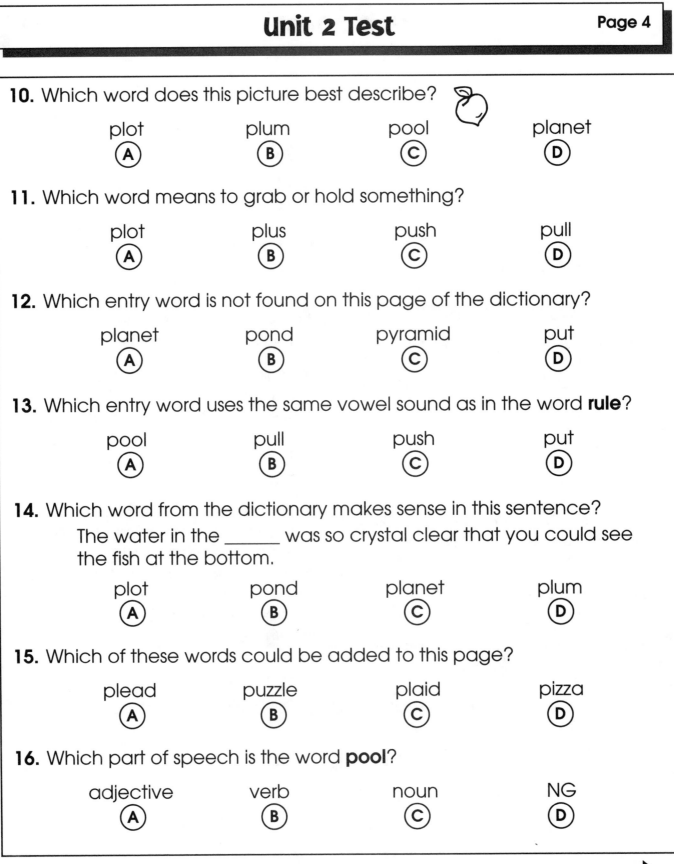

plot      plum      pool      planet
(A)         (B)        (C)        (D)

**11.** Which word means to grab or hold something?

plot      plus      push      pull
(A)         (B)        (C)        (D)

**12.** Which entry word is not found on this page of the dictionary?

planet      pond      pyramid      put
(A)         (B)        (C)        (D)

**13.** Which entry word uses the same vowel sound as in the word **rule**?

pool      pull      push      put
(A)         (B)        (C)        (D)

**14.** Which word from the dictionary makes sense in this sentence?
The water in the _____ was so crystal clear that you could see the fish at the bottom.

plot      pond      planet      plum
(A)         (B)        (C)        (D)

**15.** Which of these words could be added to this page?

plead      puzzle      plaid      pizza
(A)         (B)        (C)        (D)

**16.** Which part of speech is the word **pool**?

adjective      verb      noun      NG
(A)         (B)        (C)        (D)

GO ON ➤

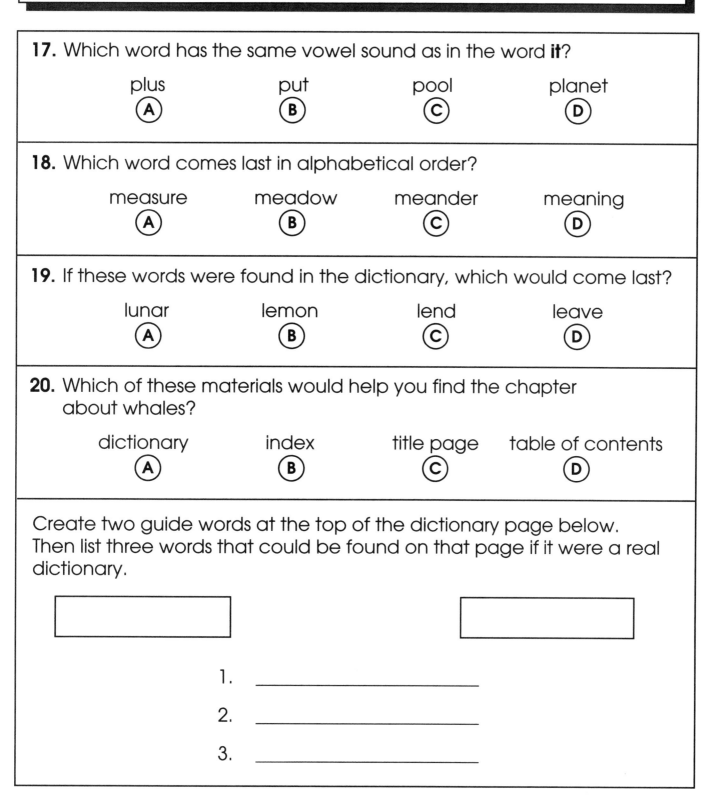

**17.** Which word has the same vowel sound as in the word **it**?

plus
(A)

put
(B)

pool
(C)

planet
(D)

**18.** Which word comes last in alphabetical order?

measure
(A)

meadow
(B)

meander
(C)

meaning
(D)

**19.** If these words were found in the dictionary, which would come last?

lunar
(A)

lemon
(B)

lend
(C)

leave
(D)

**20.** Which of these materials would help you find the chapter about whales?

dictionary
(A)

index
(B)

title page
(C)

table of contents
(D)

Create two guide words at the top of the dictionary page below.
Then list three words that could be found on that page if it were a real dictionary.

1. _____

2. _____

3. _____

## Recognizing details

Unit 3

Recognizing the details of a passage means that given specific questions, the reader can respond with precise answers.

Read each note to find details to answer the questions.

Sharla,
Your music teacher called to say that you left your math book in her room. She will leave it on the secretary's desk. Try to pick it up by 4:30.

Mom,
The carpet cleaning company called to say they are running behind. They should be here within an hour of their scheduled 2:00 time.
xxx OOO

Sam,
Your pal, Jonathan, called. He may not make it to the game, because his sister broke her arm and they're still at the hospital. He said you should ask Will to play goalie if he doesn't make it.

Dad,
Uncle Joe called to say that he will meet you at the golf course after lunch rather than at the restaurant.

1. What type of book did Sharla leave behind? _____

2. Where will Uncle Joe be meeting Dad? _____

3. The carpet cleaners should be here by when? _____

4. What position does Jonathan play? _____

5. Who broke an arm? _____

6. By what time should Sharla pick up her book? _____

7. Who should Sam ask to play goalie? _____

8. Will the carpet cleaners be early or late? _____

## Recognizing details
Unit 3

Some details are harder to find because they are hidden as descriptive words (adjectives and adverbs). When you are reading for details, pay close attention to the describing words.

Use details from the passage to complete the puzzle.

### Mark Spitz: The Speedy Swimmer

Mark Spitz is an American swimmer who set an Olympic record when he won seven gold medals at the 1972 Summer Olympics in Germany. Mark had been swimming races since he was eight years old. By his late teens, he had already broken three world records in the freestyle and butterfly races. At the 1968 Olympics in Mexico, Mark hoped to win the gold medal, but he did not swim his best. He finished second in the butterfly and third in the freestyle. With heavy training, Mark Spitz came to the 1972 Olympics ready to swim his best. And did he ever!

**Across**

2. How old was Mark when he began swimming races?

3. Where were the Olympics held when Mark won seven gold medals?

5. Which stroke was Mark's best at the Olympics in Mexico?

7. Where were the Olympics held when Mark did not swim his best?

**Down**

1. How many world records did Mark set as a teenager?

4. What country did Mark represent?

6. How many gold medals did Mark win in 1972?

Name

## Understanding the main idea

The **main idea** of a passage tells what the whole passage is about. It does not tell one part of the passage or recall one fact from the passage. It is the overview for the entire passage or paragraph. Titles often tell you something about the main idea.

Which title describes the passage below?     "Tall Buildings in the U.S."     "The Sears Tower"

The Sears Tower is the world's tallest building. It is even taller than the Empire State Building in New York City. The Sears Tower has 110 stories and is 1,707 feet tall including its antenna towers on top. When the sky is clear, visitors on top of the building can see into four states!

The best title is "The Sears Tower" because the whole passage is about the Sears Tower. The Empire State Building is mentioned, but only to compare it with the Sears Tower.

The titles below describe the main idea for each passage on page 33. Write each title at the top of its partner passage. Remember to ask yourself, "Does this title tell about the whole passage?"

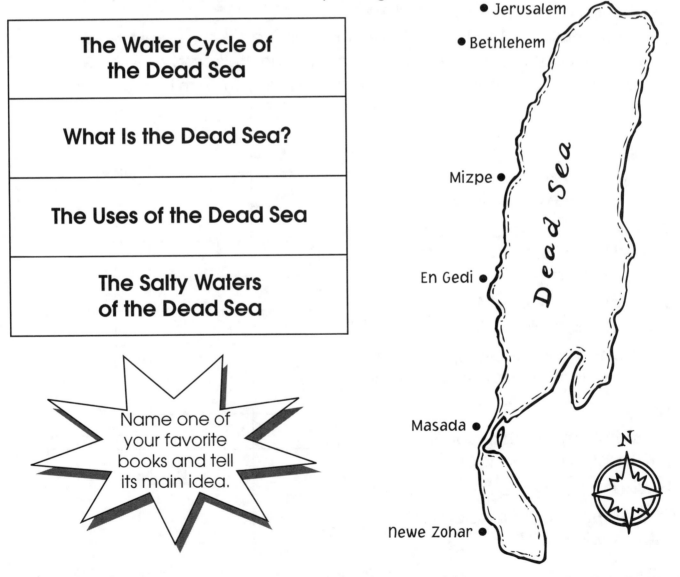

| The Water Cycle of the Dead Sea |
| What Is the Dead Sea? |
| The Uses of the Dead Sea |
| The Salty Waters of the Dead Sea |

Name one of your favorite books and tell its main idea.

Jerusalem
Bethlehem
Mizpe
En Gedi
Masada
Newe Zohar
Dead Sea
N

Name

## Understanding the main idea

See directions on page 32.

---

_____

_____

1.     The Dead Sea is a saltwater lake in Asia between Jordan and Israel. The northern part of the lake is the deepest, measuring about 2,622 feet below sea level. At the southern end of the Dead Sea is a shallow area partly cut off by a peninsula.

---

_____

_____

2.     The Dead Sea is nearly nine times more salty than the ocean! The salt is so thick that very little plant or animal life can survive in its waters. It is believed to have gotten its name for this reason. The salt is also thick enough that if a person tries to swim in the Dead Sea, he floats on top!

---

3.     The Dead Sea is valuable for a couple of reasons. Its salt is mined easily and inexpensively. Its waters are used for beauty and health reasons. Many queens, kings, and famous people have been to the sea for health or beauty reasons. Thousands of people still visit the sea in hopes of curing skin and bone troubles.

4.     The Dead Sea gets its water from a river to the north called the Jordan River, which empties into the sea. Other smaller streams also feed water into the Dead Sea, mostly from the east side. There are no rivers that lead out of the sea, so the water stays in place until it evaporates. Because the Dead Sea is located in the desert, evaporation is fast!

---

## Discovering topic sentences

Longer passages may be written in paragraphs, each telling about something different. In this case the title should be about the entire passage. Each paragraph will have a topic sentence that tells about the main idea.

Choose a title to describe the main idea of the entire passage below. Then choose the topic sentence for each paragraph. Circle your answers.

Lobsters are saltwater animals belonging to a group called crustaceans. They have a hard outer shell and five sets of legs. The first set of legs are known as claws. One is usually used for crushing and the other for biting. The female lays thousands of eggs, and the tiny young drift and swim for three to five weeks before settling on the bottom of the ocean.

Crayfish are freshwater versions of their crustacean cousins called lobsters. Crawfish, as they are also called, may be as short as two inches in length. Like their cousins, crayfish have large front claws that are actually one of five sets of legs. Crayfish are found around the world in freshwater rivers and streams except in Africa and Antarctica.

1. A good title for this story would be:

   A. River Animals

   B. Lobsters

   C. Cousins with Claws

2. The topic sentence in paragraph 1 is:

   A. The first set of legs are known as claws.

   B. They have a hard outer shell and five sets of legs.

   C. Lobsters are saltwater animals belonging to a group called crustaceans.

3. The topic sentence in paragraph 2 is:

   A. Crawfish, as they are also called, may be as short as two inches in length.

   B. Crayfish are freshwater versions of their crustacean cousins called lobsters.

   C. Crayfish are found in freshwater rivers and streams.

Name

The **supporting details** are the parts of a paragraph that tell more about the topic sentence. They describe the main idea in more detail. The underlined phrases below are supporting details.

Jeffrey was having a great day until his mom told him that he had to share his pet snake with his sister. He knew that <u>Lana would scream and scare his new best friend</u>. Besides, Lana had been playing dress-up, and <u>she smelled like a perfume bottle</u>. No pet snake should have to smell like that.

In each paragraph below, circle the topic sentence and underline two supporting details.

1.  Some people like the fire department across the street from our neighborhood, and some people do not. My mom and dad think it is great because they know that help could reach us within minutes. Nan's parents do not like it because of all the noise the sirens make. I guess I can see both sides.

2.  Every evening, Gabriel and his dad look forward to feeding the deer in their backyard. Gabriel carries the dried corn from the garage to the edge of the woods. He and his dad spread the corn, then hide behind the edge of the house to watch. Each evening, the same four female deer come to feed. Maybe someday they will have a newcomer!

3.  Alley worked hard to finish all of her projects at summer camp. She tie-dyed her shirt in shades of blue and purple, glued eyes onto her lion's mask, and carefully formed a monkey out of clay. Now it was time for her favorite camp "project," lunch!

Name

## Pinpointing supporting details

Remember that supporting details give more information about the topic sentence.

Read the passage. Circle the topic sentence in each paragraph, then write two supporting details.

### Colorado Attractions

Pike's Peak is the name given to one of the mountains located in the Rocky Mountains of Colorado. It is not the highest peak in the state but is well-known for its amazing view at the top. When visiting, you can climb the mountain by horseback, cog railway, or car. Pike's Peak was named after the American explorer who discovered it in 1806.

The Royal Gorge is a deep canyon that was created by the snow and rain that run off the Rocky Mountains and into rivers. The Arkansas River runs through the bottom of the canyon, which is about 1,000 feet deep. Visitors can enjoy an awesome view from the suspension bridge, which crosses the canyon.

### PARAGRAPH 1

Supporting Detail: _____

_____

Supporting Detail: _____

_____

### PARAGRAPH 2

Supporting Detail: _____

_____

Supporting Detail: _____

_____

Name

Read or listen to the directions. Fill in the circle beside the best answer.

☐ Example:

The _____ tells what a passage is mostly about.

(A) detail

(B) paragraph

(C) main idea

(D) supporting detail

Read all of the answer choices before you decide.

Answer: C because the main idea tells about the whole passage.

Now try these. You have 25 minutes. Continue until you see ⬡STOP.

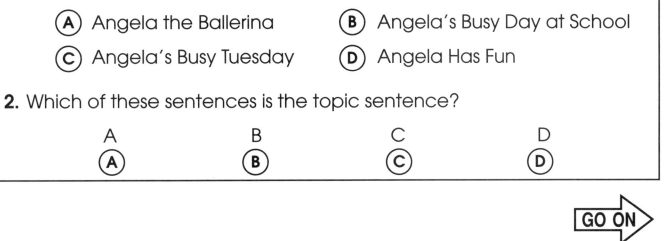

Use the passage to answer questions 1–4.

Tuesdays are busy for Angela (A). She gets up early for swim practice, which starts at 7:30 (B). Then her mom drops her off just as the morning bell rings (C). After the bus brings her home, Angela grabs a quick snack before she leaves for dance lessons (D). Angela says she loves all of her activities, but she always eats a great dinner and hits the sack early on Tuesday nights!

1. Which of these would make a good title for the passage?

(A) Angela the Ballerina

(B) Angela's Busy Day at School

(C) Angela's Busy Tuesday

(D) Angela Has Fun

2. Which of these sentences is the topic sentence?

A (A)    B (B)    C (C)    D (D)

GO ON ⟩

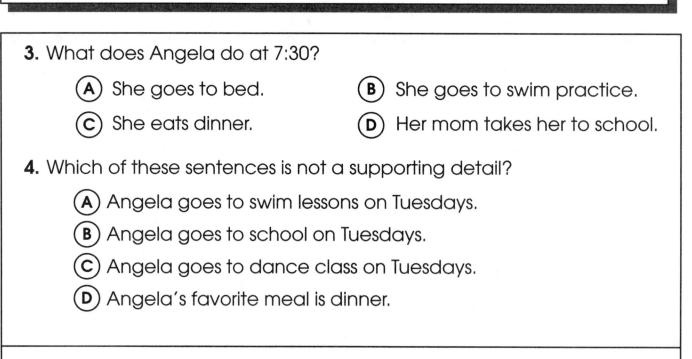

**3.** What does Angela do at 7:30?

(A) She goes to bed.   (B) She goes to swim practice.

(C) She eats dinner.   (D) Her mom takes her to school.

**4.** Which of these sentences is not a supporting detail?

(A) Angela goes to swim lessons on Tuesdays.

(B) Angela goes to school on Tuesdays.

(C) Angela goes to dance class on Tuesdays.

(D) Angela's favorite meal is dinner.

Use the passage below to answer questions 5–9.

All around the world, castles, or fortresses, have been built with one goal in mind: to protect countries' royal leaders from their enemies. The first castles were usually built on hills and were nothing more than wooden buildings. If the land was flat, workers moved land to make a hill for the site of the castle, serving as a lookout. Soon, walls were added to surround the area along with moats and drawbridges to discourage enemies from attacking.

Later, castles became even better prepared for battle. They were often built on the edge of a cliff where enemy attacks could be seen ahead of time. Tall towers with thick walls and small windows were added to serve as lookouts and as storage for food, water, and supplies. The tower was the strongest part of the castle, so it often became the last safe place to run in a losing battle.

Many castles still exist today. Some are in ruins, which means they have fallen down or lost important parts like their roofs. Several others have been repaired and are now museums that are open to visitors. Still other castles are actually serving as homes!

GO ON

**5.** Which of these would not make a good title for this passage?

(A) Kings and Queens       (B) Castles

(C) Fortresses       (D) What Is a Castle?

**6.** Where were the supplies kept in a castle?

(A) the moat       (B) the drawbridge

(C) the tower       (D) the cliff

**7.** Which of these is the topic sentence of the second paragraph?

(A) Castles were often built on the edge of a cliff.

(B) Later, castles became even better prepared for battle.

(C) Tall towers with thick walls and small windows were added to serve as lookouts.

(D) All around the world, castles, or fortresses, have been built to protect their owners.

**8.** Which of these ideas does not support the topic sentence of the first paragraph?

(A) Many castles are now museums.

(B) The first castles were built on hills so armies could see the enemy coming.

(C) They started building moats to make it hard for enemies to reach the castle.

(D) If the land was flat, workers moved land to make a hill.

GO ON

**9.** What are ruins in the passage?

(A) the supplies needed for battle

(B) the highest part of the tower

(C) the king and queen

(D) the castles that have fallen down

**10.** Which detail does not describe the main idea?

Nicki was nervous about her dance on stage. Her knees were shaking, she was wearing make-up, she had butterflies in her stomach, and she felt funny.

(A) Her knees were shaking.

(B) She was wearing make-up.

(C) She had butterflies in her stomach.

(D) She felt funny.

**11.** Given this topic sentence, which of the details would you not expect to find in the same paragraph?

Learning tae kwon do takes a lot of concentration.

(A) You must listen closely to your master.

(B) You must follow directions.

(C) You must use kicks and punches only in class.

(D) You must tie a belt around your waist.

GO ON

# Unit 3 Test

**12.** Your teacher has asked you to write a story about your life from the time you were born up to now. What might you name it?

(A) My Baby Days

(B) My First Bike

(C) My Family

(D) My Life

Use the poem to answer questions 13–15.

**An Animal's Smile** by Lisa Molengraft

The beaver, the elephant, the scaly crocodile—
Have you wondered what's behind an animal's smile?

A horse's set of pearly whites are square and rather flat.
They grind the grass the animal eats. Is there anything better than that?

Walruses' tusks are actually teeth that hang very long.
They use their teeth for fighting, not for chewing or singing a song.

Crocodiles have sharp teeth they use to catch their prey.
So if you see a crocodile coming, be sure to run away.

Sharp teeth, long teeth, teeth that are square—
Though they all look different, animal teeth are everywhere!

**13.** What is the poem mostly about?

(A) Animals eat meat.

(B) Animals' teeth have many uses.

(C) Animals need to take care of their teeth.

(D) Animals use their teeth to fight.

**14.** Walruses use their teeth to

(A) protect themselves.

(B) catch their prey.

(C) chew.

(D) make sounds.

GO ON

**15.** Which of these does not support the main idea?

(A) Many animals have teeth.

(B) Animals use their teeth differently.

(C) Animal teeth can look very different.

(D) Stay away from crocodiles.

Read the passage below to answer questions 16–20.

The platypus is considered by some to be a misfit mammal. It has fur and is warmblooded as you would expect in a mammal, but the platypus lays eggs like a bird! It also has webbed feet and a rounded bill like a duck. The platypus lives along streams in Australia where it can find plenty of shellfish, worms, and insects. Even the platypus's meals seem more suited to a bird than a mammal. This must be a confused animal!

**16.** Which of these is the main idea of the passage?

(A) The platypus has fur.

(B) The platypus lays eggs.

(C) The platypus is a mammal with some bird-like traits.

(D) The platypus is a bird with some mammal-like traits.

**17.** Why does the platypus have webbed feet?

(A) to help him fly south for winter

(B) to help him swim and catch food

(C) to help him run more quickly

(D) to help him clean himself

GO ON

**42**

**18.** Which of these details does not support the main idea?

(A) The platypus has a duck-like bill.

(B) The platypus lays eggs like a bird.

(C) The platypus is a friendly animal.

(D) The platypus is a mammal.

**19.** Which of these is not part of the platypus's diet?

seaweed (A)  worms (B)  shellfish (C)  bugs (D)

**20.** Which of these would make a good title for the passage?

(A) Strange Birds

(B) Mammals Around the World

(C) Mammals Lay Eggs

(D) A Bird-Like Mammal

Read the paragraph for details, then label each bus with its number.

It is time for school to end. There are five buses in front of the school. Number 10 is last in line. Number 20 is behind number 30. Number 40 is behind number 20. Number 50 is behind Number 40.

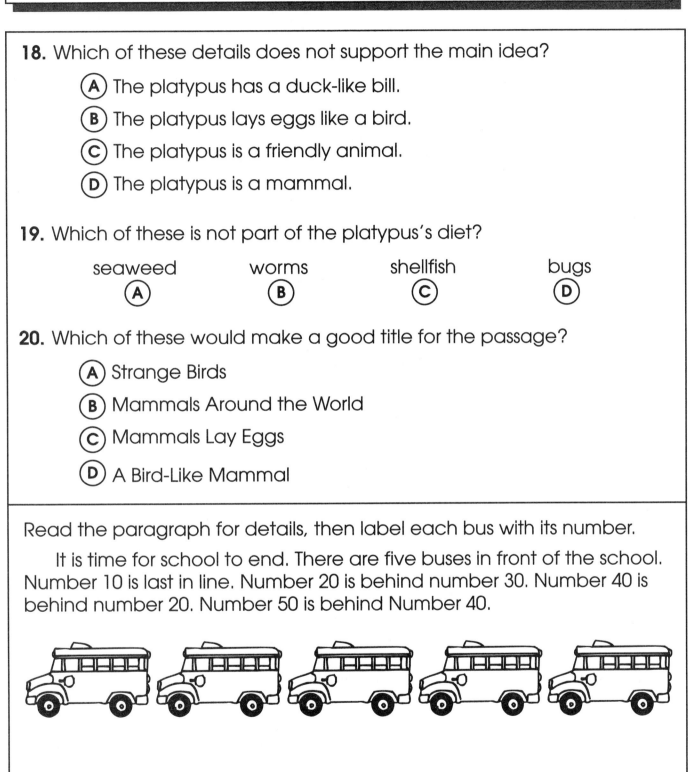

STOP

Name

## Understanding a sequence

Using **sequence** means putting events in the order in which they happened.
Sequencing will provide order and help you make sense of what you read.

Reading a chart helps you see the order of events more clearly. Use the chart below to find the answers.

## Our Day at Animal World

| 10:45–11:15 | The Reptile Review |
| 11:20–11:45 | Elsie the Elephant Show |
| 11:45–12:15 | Lunch at the Penguin Palace |
| 12:30–1:00 | Sea Lion Show |
| 1:10–1:35 | Birds of Prey |
| 2:00–4:45 | The Monkey Movie |
| 5:00–6:00 | Dinner at the Coyote Cafe |
| 6:10–6:25 | Wildcat Wackiness |
| 6:30–7:00 | Penguins on Parade |

1. Which show is right after the Sea Lion Show? _____

2. Will you eat lunch before or after the Elephant Show? _____

3. Which shows will you see after dinner? _____

   and _____

4. Which show is before the Elephant Show? _____

5. What will you be doing at 3:00? _____

6. Where will you eat lunch? _____

Name

## Using key sequencing words

Key words are often used to give you clues about the sequence of a story's events. Words like *first*, *then*, *next*, and *last* are examples of such words.

Use the key words to help you decide which sentence comes first. Label the sentences **1st** and **2nd**. Then underline the key words that helped you decide.

1. ____ Before, I walked to school.

   ____ Now, I take the bus to school.

2. ____ Football practice starts soon.

   ____ School starts immediately.

3. ____ First, you need to clean your room.

   ____ Next, you need to fold your clothes.

4. ____ She did her math homework earlier.

   ____ She is finally doing her spelling homework.

5. ____ We need to get to swim lessons right away.

   ____ We need to get to piano lessons eventually.

6. ____ My parents said that we will get a puppy someday.

   ____ My parents said that we will get a fish soon.

7. ____ My mom says that I will learn to like asparagus eventually.

   ____ My mom says that I will never learn to like broccoli.

8. ____ My teacher will send my test scores home later.

   ____ My teacher will send my report card home immediately.

## Comprehending a sequence

Unit 4

The sequence of a story can be imagined as you read it. Watch for key words to help you remember the order of important events.

Number the sentences from 1–6 to retell the story in sequence.

# The Midnight Ride

It was early morning on April 19, 1775. Paul Revere and many other colonists were ready to fight against the British king's army. They called themselves minutemen because they would have to be ready to fight at a minute's notice. First, Paul waited for a signal from the American spies. They knew the British army would eventually move toward Lexington and Concord, but they were unsure whether the British would travel by land or across the water. When Paul received word, he would send a signal to the other minutemen telling them which direction the British were attacking. Next, he would ride his horse quickly through the farmland and towns shouting the news that the British were coming.

At last, the word came from the spies. Paul immediately ordered two lanterns to be hung in the tall tower of the church, a signal that meant the British were attacking by boat. Then he mounted his horse and rode fast into the night. Paul Revere knew the importance of warning the minutemen to prepare for battle. The British army had more men and more guns, so the minutemen would have to surprise them. Paul rode through Lexington, shouting the news. But as he rode out of town, he was caught by the British. Meanwhile, two other riders made it further and told the minutemen to be ready to fight in Concord.

Soon, the British army reached Concord. They had no idea the minutemen were waiting. They were surprised and fled the area. The minutemen that were awakened had won their first fight and someday there would be freedom.

Paul Revere was caught by a British soldier.

Two lanterns were lit in the church tower.

Paul Revere rode through Lexington.

The minutemen surprised the British army in Concord.

Paul Revere received word from the spies.

Two other American riders warned the minutemen to gather in Concord.

Name

## Understanding cause and effect

Many stories add a cause and effect to help you understand why something has happened in the story. Think about the story "Little Red Riding Hood."

Effect (what happened) — Little Red Riding Hood thought her grandma looked strange.

Cause (what made it happen) — It was really the wolf dressed up!

Read the effects below. Find the cause for each and write the matching letter on the line.

_____ 1. The house was a mess! Magazines and newspapers had been torn to pieces, and the bag of dog food was spilled all over the kitchen floor.

_____ 2. The team had finished warming up, and it was time for the game to begin. "How can we start without our pitcher?" the team wondered. "Where is he?"

_____ 3. We would have to drive more slowly than we had expected.

_____ 4. When her mom called her for dinner, she almost felt sick. "I cannot eat a thing," she said.

A. As we approached the shore, the fog became so thick we could hardly see in front of us. Mom turned on the lights and told us to settle in.

B. Jamie's mom was not around when she got home from school. Jamie helped herself to a handful of pretzels and a bowl of ice cream. Then she found the cookies her mom had baked.

C. Billy had promised to go straight home after school to take care of his dog. Then Billy's neighbor invited him to play a quick game of basketball on their way home. "Okay," he agreed.

D. "Mom, can I spend the night at Chase's house?" Carlos asked. "Carlos, you have an early game tomorrow," she answered. "That's okay, Mom, I won't be too tired," Carlos begged.

Discuss with an adult how day and night happens. Record the cause and effect.

## Finding the cause

Many of the events in a story are caused by something else. Watch for clues that tell you about the cause.

Use the story to answer the questions.

# The Vanishing School Supplies

"Mom, I need more pencils for school tomorrow. I think I should get a lot," Timothy said as he jumped in the car.

"Wow, you must really be working hard. You have used so many school supplies already. Last week you needed scissors and the week before that it was markers," replied Timothy's mother.

The next morning, Timothy packed two packs of brand new pencils in his backpack. When his mother picked him up, Timothy said, "Hey, Mom, can we swing by the store to get more colored pencils?"

"What?" Timothy's mother asked. "Timothy Arnold, what is going on? You cannot possibly be using all your supplies this quickly."

"Well, I am sharing them. It all started when Gerald made fun of Pete's pencil. It was almost completely used up and the eraser was totally gone. It looked pretty bad. Then Pete said that his family could not buy any more pencils until his dad got paid again. So I started thinking about it and realized that Pete never had his own scissors or markers, so I gave him mine."

"Timothy, I am very proud of you. I have an idea. Let's invite Pete to get ice cream with us after school tomorrow. I think the two of you could learn a lot from each other."

1. Why did Timothy ask for so many new supplies? _____

_____

2. Why did not Pete have his own school supplies? _____

_____

3. Why did Gerald make fun of Pete's pencil? _____

_____

4. Why did Timothy's mom feel proud of her son? _____

_____

Name

Read or listen to the directions. Fill in the circle beside the best answer.

❏ Example:

Which of these happened first?

(A) Sooner or later I will walk to the library.

(B) Eventually I will go to the store.

(C) First, I need to go to school.

(D) Someday, I will go to the football game.

Watch for key words in the story that give you clues.

Answer: C because the key word first tells that it happened first.

Now try these. You have 25 minutes. Continue until you see (STOP).

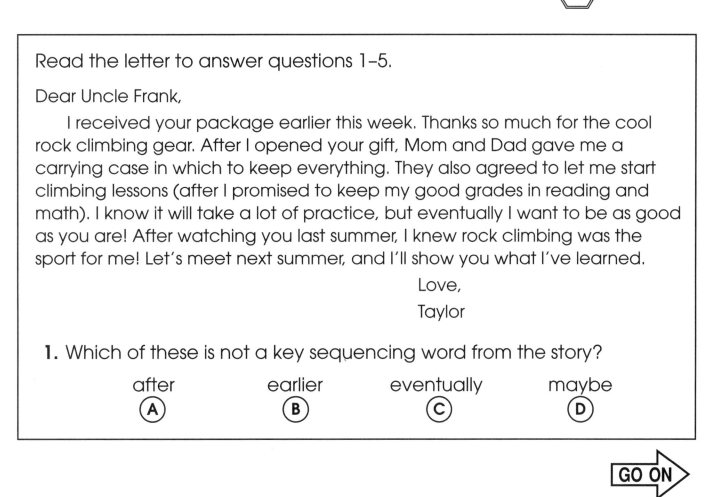

Read the letter to answer questions 1–5.

Dear Uncle Frank,

   I received your package earlier this week. Thanks so much for the cool rock climbing gear. After I opened your gift, Mom and Dad gave me a carrying case in which to keep everything. They also agreed to let me start climbing lessons (after I promised to keep my good grades in reading and math). I know it will take a lot of practice, but eventually I want to be as good as you are! After watching you last summer, I knew rock climbing was the sport for me! Let's meet next summer, and I'll show you what I've learned.

                              Love,

                              Taylor

**1.** Which of these is not a key sequencing word from the story?

after          earlier          eventually          maybe
(A)            (B)              (C)                 (D)

GO ON ▷

**2.** Why did Taylor want to learn to rock climb?

(A) He had seen his uncle climb.

(B) He had seen climbing on TV.

(C) He just wanted the gear.

(D) He had seen his mom and dad climb.

**3.** Which of these did not happen before Taylor wrote this letter?

(A) Taylor watched Uncle Frank rock climb.

(B) Taylor received Uncle Frank's package.

(C) Taylor took rock climbing lessons.

(D) Taylor's mom and dad gave him a carrying case.

**4.** Why did Taylor promise to keep good grades?

(A) So he could get rock climbing gear.

(B) So he could go climbing with his uncle.

(C) So he could take climbing lessons.

(D) So he would not be in trouble.

**5.** If the boxes to the right are in sequence, which sentence belongs in the empty box?

(A) Taylor decided he wanted to learn to rock climb.

(B) Taylor's parents agreed to lessons.

(C) Taylor watched his uncle rock climb.

(D) Taylor's parents gave him a carrying case.

GO ON

Read the story to answer questions 6–12.

Finally, September 24 had arrived! This year's Farmington Fall Festival was going to be the best ever. Everyone had a job to do. Suzy picked and washed the apples, while Laura stacked the pumpkins into baskets. Their other classmates were busy piling bales of hay for stuffing scarecrows. Mr. Higgins had hooked the wagon to the back of the tractor for hayrides. Things were going just as planned.

Joey and James had a job to do as well. They were in charge of getting the apples, pumpkins, and hay to the festival grounds. These supplies were not needed yet, so the boys knew they had extra time on their hands. They decided to go fishing for a while first. What great luck they were having! Joey hooked the largest catfish he had ever seen, and James's hook was working like a fish magnet.

Three hours later, the Farmington Fall Festival was well underway. Sharina had won the pie-eating contest, and Luke Barrington's family was about to take the blue ribbon in the potato sack race. However, everyone was disappointed there was no apple-bobbing contest or pumpkin-carving booth. And why had the hayrides not started yet?

Suzy, Laura, and their classmates could not believe it. After all their hard work, the apples, pumpkins, and hay never made it to the festival.

6. Why weren't the apples, pumpkins, and hay at the festival?

(A) Joey and James forgot about their job.

(B) Joey and James were angry at the others.

(C) Joey and James were busy with the potato sack race.

(D) Joey and James did not think they needed them yet.

7. What does it mean that James's hook was working like a magnet?

(A) The fish were not biting.　(B) He was catching many fish.

(C) It was made of metal.　(D) The fish were circling around.

**8.** Why did the boys have extra time on their hands?

(A) They did not know about the festival.

(B) They did not want to help.

(C) Their job came after everyone else's.

(D) Their jobs were already done.

**9.** Which of these events happened last in the story?

(A) Sharina won the pie-eating contest.

(B) Luke Barrington's family won the potato sack race.

(C) Mr. Higgins hooked the wagon to the back of the tractor.

(D) Suzy picked and washed apples.

**10.** How did James and Joey cause the others to feel?

(A) They were probably angry.

(B) They may have felt sorry for their friends.

(C) They probably missed James and Joey.

(D) They probably did not care.

**11.** Which sentence would fit into the empty box to show the sequence?

| Joey and James had extra time. | → | | → | The Farmington Fall Festival began. |

(A) The classmates worked hard to bale hay.

(B) The boys forgot about the festival.

(C) Suzy, Laura, and the others could not believe the apples, pumpkins, and hay were not at the festival.

(D) Laura stacked the pumpkins.

**12.** What caused James and Joey to forget their job?

(A) They were piling bales of hay.

(B) They were having fun swimming.

(C) They were washing apples and stacking pumpkins.

(D) They were having good luck fishing.

**13.** What is the most likely cause for this effect?

The crowd in the stands jumped to their feet and waved their arms.

(A) Their team had just scored a touchdown.

(B) A plane was flying overhead.

(C) A swarm of bees was attacking.

(D) They saw someone they knew.

For questions 14–17, choose the letters to show the sequence of the events.

A. Mom got us popcorn and candy as the movie started.

B. We read the book <u>Atlantis</u> before we saw the movie.

C. The movie should be out on video and DVD later.

D. The last part of the movie really surprised me.

**14.** First,

(A) (B)

(C) (D)

**15.** Then

(A) (B)

(C) (D)

**16.** Next,

(A) (B)

(C) (D)

**17.** Last,

(A) (B)

(C) (D)

GO ON

**18.** Which of these key words would tell the last thing to happen?

immediately
(A)

shortly
(B)

first
(C)

eventually
(D)

Read the recipe to answer questions 19 and 20.

### Grandma's Buckeyes

<u>Ingredients</u>

12-ounce bag of chocolate chips
1 cup of crushed graham crackers
2 cups of powdered sugar
1 stick of butter
1 cup of crunchy peanut butter

<u>Directions</u>

1. Melt the butter.

2. Mix all of the ingredients together except the chocolate chips.

3. Roll the dough into balls.

4. Place the balls on a cookie sheet.

5. Put them in the freezer for 15 minutes to help them harden.

6. Melt the bag of chocolate chips.

7. Dip the balls in the chocolate, then freeze them for another 2 hours.

**19.** Which of these should be done first?

(A) Melt the butter.

(B) Melt the bag of chocolate chips.

(C) Crush the graham crackers.

(D) Freeze the balls for 2 hours.

GO ON

**20.** Why do you need to freeze the balls before you put the chocolate on them?

(A) So the chocolate will not melt them.

(B) So the chocolate will stick to them.

(C) So they are ball-shaped.

(D) So they will harden.

Write about three things you did today. Use a sentence to tell about each and include a key sequencing word in each sentence.

1. _____

_____

2. _____

_____

3. _____

_____

# Midway Review Test Name Grid

Write your name in pencil in the boxes along the top. Begin with your last name. Fill in as many letters as will fit. Then follow the columns straight down and bubble in the letters that correspond with the letters in your name. Complete the rest of the information the same way. You may use a piece of scrap paper to help you keep your place.

| STUDENT'S NAME | | | | | | | | | | | | | | | | | |
|---|---|---|---|---|---|---|---|---|---|---|---|---|---|---|---|---|---|
| LAST | | | | | | | | | | | FIRST | | | | | | MI |
| | | | | | | | | | | | | | | | | | |
| ○ | ○ | ○ | ○ | ○ | ○ | ○ | ○ | ○ | ○ | ○ | ○ | ○ | ○ | ○ | ○ | ○ | ○ |
| Ⓐ | Ⓐ | Ⓐ | Ⓐ | Ⓐ | Ⓐ | Ⓐ | Ⓐ | Ⓐ | Ⓐ | Ⓐ | Ⓐ | Ⓐ | Ⓐ | Ⓐ | Ⓐ | Ⓐ | Ⓐ |
| Ⓑ | Ⓑ | Ⓑ | Ⓑ | Ⓑ | Ⓑ | Ⓑ | Ⓑ | Ⓑ | Ⓑ | Ⓑ | Ⓑ | Ⓑ | Ⓑ | Ⓑ | Ⓑ | Ⓑ | Ⓑ |
| Ⓒ | Ⓒ | Ⓒ | Ⓒ | Ⓒ | Ⓒ | Ⓒ | Ⓒ | Ⓒ | Ⓒ | Ⓒ | Ⓒ | Ⓒ | Ⓒ | Ⓒ | Ⓒ | Ⓒ | Ⓒ |
| Ⓓ | Ⓓ | Ⓓ | Ⓓ | Ⓓ | Ⓓ | Ⓓ | Ⓓ | Ⓓ | Ⓓ | Ⓓ | Ⓓ | Ⓓ | Ⓓ | Ⓓ | Ⓓ | Ⓓ | Ⓓ |
| Ⓔ | Ⓔ | Ⓔ | Ⓔ | Ⓔ | Ⓔ | Ⓔ | Ⓔ | Ⓔ | Ⓔ | Ⓔ | Ⓔ | Ⓔ | Ⓔ | Ⓔ | Ⓔ | Ⓔ | Ⓔ |
| Ⓕ | Ⓕ | Ⓕ | Ⓕ | Ⓕ | Ⓕ | Ⓕ | Ⓕ | Ⓕ | Ⓕ | Ⓕ | Ⓕ | Ⓕ | Ⓕ | Ⓕ | Ⓕ | Ⓕ | Ⓕ |
| Ⓖ | Ⓖ | Ⓖ | Ⓖ | Ⓖ | Ⓖ | Ⓖ | Ⓖ | Ⓖ | Ⓖ | Ⓖ | Ⓖ | Ⓖ | Ⓖ | Ⓖ | Ⓖ | Ⓖ | Ⓖ |
| Ⓗ | Ⓗ | Ⓗ | Ⓗ | Ⓗ | Ⓗ | Ⓗ | Ⓗ | Ⓗ | Ⓗ | Ⓗ | Ⓗ | Ⓗ | Ⓗ | Ⓗ | Ⓗ | Ⓗ | Ⓗ |
| Ⓘ | Ⓘ | Ⓘ | Ⓘ | Ⓘ | Ⓘ | Ⓘ | Ⓘ | Ⓘ | Ⓘ | Ⓘ | Ⓘ | Ⓘ | Ⓘ | Ⓘ | Ⓘ | Ⓘ | Ⓘ |
| Ⓙ | Ⓙ | Ⓙ | Ⓙ | Ⓙ | Ⓙ | Ⓙ | Ⓙ | Ⓙ | Ⓙ | Ⓙ | Ⓙ | Ⓙ | Ⓙ | Ⓙ | Ⓙ | Ⓙ | Ⓙ |
| Ⓚ | Ⓚ | Ⓚ | Ⓚ | Ⓚ | Ⓚ | Ⓚ | Ⓚ | Ⓚ | Ⓚ | Ⓚ | Ⓚ | Ⓚ | Ⓚ | Ⓚ | Ⓚ | Ⓚ | Ⓚ |
| Ⓛ | Ⓛ | Ⓛ | Ⓛ | Ⓛ | Ⓛ | Ⓛ | Ⓛ | Ⓛ | Ⓛ | Ⓛ | Ⓛ | Ⓛ | Ⓛ | Ⓛ | Ⓛ | Ⓛ | Ⓛ |
| Ⓜ | Ⓜ | Ⓜ | Ⓜ | Ⓜ | Ⓜ | Ⓜ | Ⓜ | Ⓜ | Ⓜ | Ⓜ | Ⓜ | Ⓜ | Ⓜ | Ⓜ | Ⓜ | Ⓜ | Ⓜ |
| Ⓝ | Ⓝ | Ⓝ | Ⓝ | Ⓝ | Ⓝ | Ⓝ | Ⓝ | Ⓝ | Ⓝ | Ⓝ | Ⓝ | Ⓝ | Ⓝ | Ⓝ | Ⓝ | Ⓝ | Ⓝ |
| Ⓞ | Ⓞ | Ⓞ | Ⓞ | Ⓞ | Ⓞ | Ⓞ | Ⓞ | Ⓞ | Ⓞ | Ⓞ | Ⓞ | Ⓞ | Ⓞ | Ⓞ | Ⓞ | Ⓞ | Ⓞ |
| Ⓟ | Ⓟ | Ⓟ | Ⓟ | Ⓟ | Ⓟ | Ⓟ | Ⓟ | Ⓟ | Ⓟ | Ⓟ | Ⓟ | Ⓟ | Ⓟ | Ⓟ | Ⓟ | Ⓟ | Ⓟ |
| Ⓠ | Ⓠ | Ⓠ | Ⓠ | Ⓠ | Ⓠ | Ⓠ | Ⓠ | Ⓠ | Ⓠ | Ⓠ | Ⓠ | Ⓠ | Ⓠ | Ⓠ | Ⓠ | Ⓠ | Ⓠ |
| Ⓡ | Ⓡ | Ⓡ | Ⓡ | Ⓡ | Ⓡ | Ⓡ | Ⓡ | Ⓡ | Ⓡ | Ⓡ | Ⓡ | Ⓡ | Ⓡ | Ⓡ | Ⓡ | Ⓡ | Ⓡ |
| Ⓢ | Ⓢ | Ⓢ | Ⓢ | Ⓢ | Ⓢ | Ⓢ | Ⓢ | Ⓢ | Ⓢ | Ⓢ | Ⓢ | Ⓢ | Ⓢ | Ⓢ | Ⓢ | Ⓢ | Ⓢ |
| Ⓣ | Ⓣ | Ⓣ | Ⓣ | Ⓣ | Ⓣ | Ⓣ | Ⓣ | Ⓣ | Ⓣ | Ⓣ | Ⓣ | Ⓣ | Ⓣ | Ⓣ | Ⓣ | Ⓣ | Ⓣ |
| Ⓤ | Ⓤ | Ⓤ | Ⓤ | Ⓤ | Ⓤ | Ⓤ | Ⓤ | Ⓤ | Ⓤ | Ⓤ | Ⓤ | Ⓤ | Ⓤ | Ⓤ | Ⓤ | Ⓤ | Ⓤ |
| Ⓥ | Ⓥ | Ⓥ | Ⓥ | Ⓥ | Ⓥ | Ⓥ | Ⓥ | Ⓥ | Ⓥ | Ⓥ | Ⓥ | Ⓥ | Ⓥ | Ⓥ | Ⓥ | Ⓥ | Ⓥ |
| Ⓦ | Ⓦ | Ⓦ | Ⓦ | Ⓦ | Ⓦ | Ⓦ | Ⓦ | Ⓦ | Ⓦ | Ⓦ | Ⓦ | Ⓦ | Ⓦ | Ⓦ | Ⓦ | Ⓦ | Ⓦ |
| Ⓧ | Ⓧ | Ⓧ | Ⓧ | Ⓧ | Ⓧ | Ⓧ | Ⓧ | Ⓧ | Ⓧ | Ⓧ | Ⓧ | Ⓧ | Ⓧ | Ⓧ | Ⓧ | Ⓧ | Ⓧ |
| Ⓨ | Ⓨ | Ⓨ | Ⓨ | Ⓨ | Ⓨ | Ⓨ | Ⓨ | Ⓨ | Ⓨ | Ⓨ | Ⓨ | Ⓨ | Ⓨ | Ⓨ | Ⓨ | Ⓨ | Ⓨ |
| Ⓩ | Ⓩ | Ⓩ | Ⓩ | Ⓩ | Ⓩ | Ⓩ | Ⓩ | Ⓩ | Ⓩ | Ⓩ | Ⓩ | Ⓩ | Ⓩ | Ⓩ | Ⓩ | Ⓩ | Ⓩ |

SCHOOL

TEACHER

FEMALE ○ MALE ○

| DATE OF BIRTH | | | | |
|---|---|---|---|---|
| MONTH | DAY | | YEAR | |
| | | | | |
| JAN ○ | ⓪ | ⓪ | ⓪ | ⓪ |
| FEB ○ | ① | ① | ① | ① |
| MAR ○ | ② | ② | ② | ② |
| APR ○ | ③ | ③ | ③ | ③ |
| MAY ○ | | ④ | ④ | ④ |
| JUN ○ | | ⑤ | ⑤ | ⑤ |
| JUL ○ | | ⑥ | ⑥ | ⑥ |
| AUG ○ | | ⑦ | ⑦ | ⑦ |
| SEP ○ | | ⑧ | ⑧ | ⑧ |
| OCT ○ | | ⑨ | ⑨ | ⑨ |
| NOV ○ | | | | |
| DEC ○ | | | | |

GRADE ③ ④ ⑤

# Midway Review Test Answer Sheet

Pay close attention when transferring your answers. Fill in the bubbles neatly and completely. You may use a piece of scrap paper to help you keep your place.

SAMPLES
A Ⓐ Ⓑ ● Ⓓ
B Ⓕ ● Ⓗ Ⓙ

1 Ⓐ Ⓑ Ⓒ Ⓓ
2 Ⓕ Ⓖ Ⓗ Ⓙ
3 Ⓐ Ⓑ Ⓒ Ⓓ
4 Ⓕ Ⓖ Ⓗ Ⓙ
5 Ⓐ Ⓑ Ⓒ Ⓓ
6 Ⓕ Ⓖ Ⓗ Ⓙ
7 Ⓐ Ⓑ Ⓒ Ⓓ
8 Ⓕ Ⓖ Ⓗ Ⓙ
9 Ⓐ Ⓑ Ⓒ Ⓓ
10 Ⓕ Ⓖ Ⓗ Ⓙ
11 Ⓐ Ⓑ Ⓒ Ⓓ
12 Ⓕ Ⓖ Ⓗ Ⓙ
13 Ⓐ Ⓑ Ⓒ Ⓓ
14 Ⓕ Ⓖ Ⓗ Ⓙ
15 Ⓐ Ⓑ Ⓒ Ⓓ
16 Ⓕ Ⓖ Ⓗ Ⓙ
17 Ⓐ Ⓑ Ⓒ Ⓓ
18 Ⓕ Ⓖ Ⓗ Ⓙ
19 Ⓐ Ⓑ Ⓒ Ⓓ
20 Ⓕ Ⓖ Ⓗ Ⓙ

Name

# Midway Review Test

Read or listen to the directions. Fill in the circle beside the best answer.

☐ Example:

Your teacher has asked you to write a poem about your birthday party. What might you name it?

Ⓐ The Best Cake Ever

Ⓑ My Best Friends

Ⓒ My Birthday List

Ⓓ My Surprise Party

Answer: D because the main idea is about the party.

Now try these. You have 25 minutes. Continue until you see (STOP).

Remember your Helping Hand Strategies:

1. If you are unsure, try each answer in the blank.

2. When working with a dictionary, table of contents, or index, use your finger to keep your place.

3. Read all of the answer choices before you decide.

4. Watch for key words in the story that give you clues.

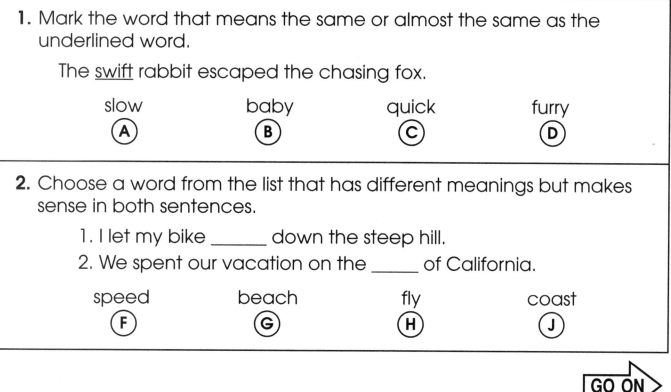

1. Mark the word that means the same or almost the same as the underlined word.

The <u>swift</u> rabbit escaped the chasing fox.

| slow | baby | quick | furry |
|------|------|-------|-------|
| Ⓐ | Ⓑ | Ⓒ | Ⓓ |

2. Choose a word from the list that has different meanings but makes sense in both sentences.

1. I let my bike _____ down the steep hill.

2. We spent our vacation on the _____ of California.

| speed | beach | fly | coast |
|-------|-------|-----|-------|
| Ⓕ | Ⓖ | Ⓗ | Ⓙ |

GO ON ⟶

Name

3. Mark the word that means the opposite of the underlined word.

Mom gave me an extra dollar in my allowance because my room looked <u>immaculate</u>.

clean          messy          busy          funny
(A)            (B)            (C)            (D)

4. Use the context of the sentence to mark the picture of a <u>sloop</u>.

As the wind grew stronger, the men struggled to get the <u>sloop</u> under control.

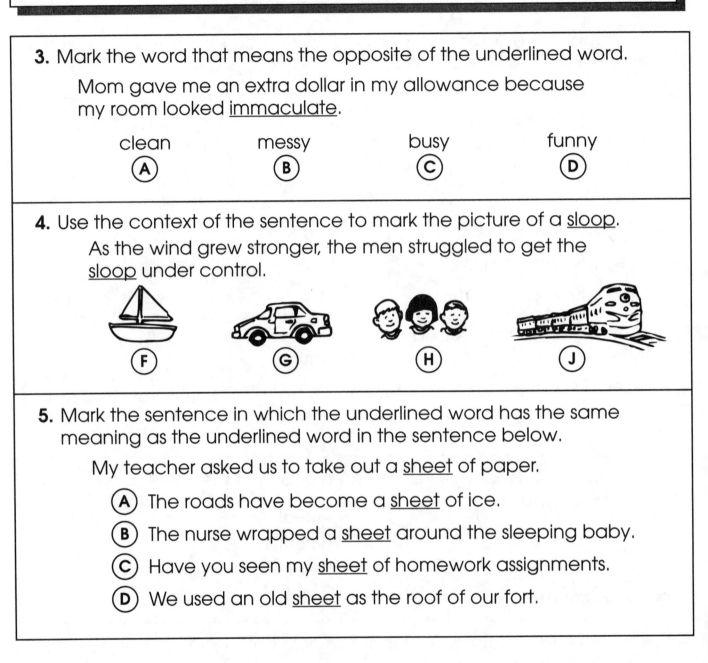

(F)          (G)          (H)          (J)

5. Mark the sentence in which the underlined word has the same meaning as the underlined word in the sentence below.

My teacher asked us to take out a <u>sheet</u> of paper.

(A) The roads have become a <u>sheet</u> of ice.

(B) The nurse wrapped a <u>sheet</u> around the sleeping baby.

(C) Have you seen my <u>sheet</u> of homework assignments.

(D) We used an old <u>sheet</u> as the roof of our fort.

GO ON

Name _____

Where would you look to find the answers to questions 6 and 7?

**Table of Contents**

**6.** How are the planes the Blue Angels fly different from the planes that the Thunderbirds fly?

| page 7 | page 18 | page 29 | page 55 |
| :---: | :---: | :---: | :---: |
| (F) | (G) | (H) | (J) |

**7.** How does the captain start the airplane's engine?

| Chapter 1 | Chapter 2 | Chapter 3 | Chapter 4 |
| :---: | :---: | :---: | :---: |
| (A) | (B) | (C) | (D) |

Use this part of a dictionary to answer questions 8–10.

**dainty** (*adjective*) — delicate

**dally** (*verb*) — delay

**damp** (*adjective*) — slightly wet

**decade** (*noun*) — ten years

**defeat$^1$** (*verb*) — to win

**defeat$^2$** (*noun*) — a loss

**distant** (*adjective*) — far away

**dolly** (*noun*) — rolling cart

**8.** Which word is a noun?

| dally | distant | dainty | dolly |
| :---: | :---: | :---: | :---: |
| (F) | (G) | (H) | (J) |

GO ON

**9.** Which word is a verb?

damp
(A)

defeat
(B)

decade
(C)

distant
(D)

**10.** Which word makes sense in the sentence below?

Mom told us to get straight home and not to _____.

dally
(F)

defeat
(G)

distant
(H)

dolly
(J)

Read the story to answer questions 11–15.

Once upon a time there was a small man who wanted to be as large as a horse. He asked the horse how he could become his size. The horse told the small man to eat many grains and run around a lot. Immediately the man did as the horse suggested, but he did not grow.

Next, the small man went to the wise owl. He remembered how the owl had helped solve previous problems. "How can I be as big as my friend the horse?" he asked.

"Why do you want to be bigger than you are?" asked the owl.

"Because if I was bigger I could win fights," the man replied right away.

"Have you ever needed or wanted to fight before?" the wise owl asked.

The man thought for a moment and soon found his answer. "Why no, I have not ever been in a fight. In fact, I do not even like fighting," the small man answered.

The wise owl smiled, "You see, you are wishing for something that you do not need," he answered. He watched as the small man walked away. He knew the man would eventually understand.

GO ON

**11.** Which of these describes the main idea?

(A) Always ask an owl for help because they are wise.

(B) Do not get in fights unless you are big.

(C) Do not bother wishing for things you do not need.

(D) If you want something, try hard to get it.

**12.** Why did the man want to be as big as a horse?

(F) He wanted to win fights.

(G) He liked eating grain and running around.

(H) He wanted to be as wise as the owl.

(J) He could not reach things.

**13.** Why did the man think the owl could help?

(A) He would understand his problem because he is small, too.

(B) He was friends with the small man and would want to help him.

(C) He had been in many fights himself.

(D) He had helped solve problems in the past.

For questions 14 and 15, choose the sentences that belong in the empty boxes to show the correct sequence.

| (14) | The man ate grains. | The small man went to visit the wise owl. | (15) | The owl told the man he didn't need to be big. |
| --- | --- | --- | --- | --- |

14.  (F) The wise owl asked why the man wanted to be bigger.

(G) The man ate grains.

(H) The man visited the horse to find out how to grow larger.

(J) The wise owl agreed to make the man bigger.

15.  (A) The wise owl asked why the man wanted to be bigger.

(B) The man ate grains.

(C) The man visited the horse to find out how to grow larger.

(D) The wise owl agreed to make the man bigger.

Name

Read the recipe to answer questions 16–20.

## Pumpkin Pie Bars

These tasty treats are as delicious as pumpkin pie, but they are much easier to pack in lunches or take along in the car. Just place them in plastic wrap and refrigerate.

### Ingredients

½ cup butter

1 cup sugar

1 teaspoon vanilla

1 ½ cups flour

1 cup milk

2 teaspoons cinnamon

15-ounce can pumpkin

¼ cup pecans (chopped)

### Directions

1. Divide the sugar into two ½ cup containers.

2. Blend butter, flour, and ½ cup sugar. Press into the bottom of a baking pan.

3. Bake at 350°F for 15 minutes until it hardens into a crust.

4. Mix pumpkin, milk, ½ cup sugar, cinnamon, and vanilla. Pour over crust.

5. Sprinkle the pecans on top of the pumpkin mixture.

6. Bake the complete mixture at 350°F for 20 minutes.

7. Cool, then cut into bars.

**16.** Why do you need to divide the sugar into two containers?

(F) You need to use ½ cup for the crust and ½ cup for the pumpkin mixture.

(G) You need to put ½ cup in the bottom of a baking pan.

(H) You need to sprinkle ½ cup on top and ½ cup on the bottom of the bars.

(J) You need to press ½ cup in the bottom of the pan and ½ cup in the crust.

**17.** What is the main idea of the beginning paragraph?

(A) These bars are better than pumpkin pie.

(B) These bars are easier to make than pumpkin pie.

(C) These bars are easier to take away from home than pumpkin pie.

(D) These bars taste better in the car.

**18.** Why do you need to bake part of the ingredients before mixing the others?

(F) to cool the bars

(G) to form a crust

(H) to bake the pecans

(J) to melt the butter

**19.** Which of these should you do first?

(A) Cool and cut into bars.

(B) Sprinkle the pecans on top of the mixture.

(C) Bake the completed mixture for 20 minutes.

(D) Bake the crust for 15 minutes.

**20.** Which of these does not need to be done before packing the bars in lunches?

(F) Cut them into bars.

(G) Place in plastic wrap.

(H) Refrigerate the bars.

(J) Spread icing on the bars.

Use a dictionary to find a word that has more than one meaning and can be used as a noun or a verb. Write the word and its two meanings.

1. _____

2. _____

STOP

## Making a reasonable inference

To make an **inference** means to sum up given information that implies something else has happened.

Example: Keisha wiped up the milk with a sponge. You can infer from the information that milk was probably spilled.

The sentences below imply that something has happened. Write a sentence telling what it may have been.

1. _____

   The boy's mom apologized to the shop owner.

2. _____

   The dog lay down by the fire to warm himself.

3. _____

   The animals scurried back into the woods.

4. _____

   The boys roared with laughter.

5. _____

   Tasha swung her bat even harder this time.

6. _____

   Marcus counted the money left in his wallet.

Name

## Making an inference involving dialogue

Unit 5

Making an inference is like being a detective. You use the information you have to think about what may have happened previously.

Use the dialogue between characters to make an inference. Write the next part of the script.

MOM: Hi, Brian. How was school today?

BRIAN: It was great. Wait until you hear about it. You are going to smile from ear to ear.

MOM: I cannot wait to hear. What happened?

BRIAN: _____

_____

_____

DAD: Sean, are you awake?

SEAN: Wow, I am so tired. I almost fell asleep right here at the baseball game.

DAD: Well, I am not surprised after last night.

SEAN: _____

_____

_____

SANDRA: What time did Tina say she will be here?

MISSY: Right after her soccer game. It should be any minute.

SANDRA: I wonder what her big surprise is. She said it definitely involves us.

MISSY: She has been very sneaky lately, and I did hear her say something about a famous rock group.

TINA: _____

_____

## Drawing conclusions

Unit 5

**Drawing conclusions** means using the information in a story to make a logical conclusion.

Read each passage. Put an **X** in the box next to each sentence that is a reasonable conclusion. Watch out! Some passages have more than one.

1.  Minnie was glad to be home after two hours of ballet practice. She could hear crickets in the woods outside her window as she turned to chapter four. Minnie could hardly wait to hear how the princess would be rescued. As she finished the chapter, she pulled the covers back to turn off the light. She burst into laughter as she looked down and realized what she was wearing.

☐ a. Minnie forgot to change out of her dance tutu.

☐ b. Minnie had already washed her face.

☐ c. Minnie stayed up past her bedtime.

☐ d. Minnie had read part of the book before.

2.  Murphy's mom quickly pulled everything out of the dryer. Then she lifted the lid of the washer, looked inside, and shook her head. She looked around the kitchen and family room, then she rushed upstairs. "I cannot find them," she called to Murphy. "The last time I saw them was after your game on Saturday. We have got to find them before 4:00!"

☐ a. Murphy's mom has friends coming over at 4:00.

☐ b. Murphy's mom is looking for Murphy's football pants.

☐ c. Murphy has a game today at 4:00.

☐ d. Murphy's mom lost her purse.

3.  Tia slowly walked to the end of the board and looked down at the water. She wanted to jump, but her feet would not cooperate. She turned and walked back, then down the ladder. "Next time," she told herself.

☐ a. Tia's friends can jump off the diving board.

☐ b. Tia is taking swim lessons.

☐ c. Tia wants to jump.

☐ d. Tia is nervous.

## Drawing conclusions in literature

Unit 5

In the book <u>Miss Nelson Is Missing</u>, a classroom teacher must help her students learn a lesson about manners, but she uses a creative approach. Watch for clues as you read this summary of the book written and illustrated by Henry Allard and James Marshall (Houghton Mifflin Company, 1977).

The students in Miss Nelson's class were acting up again. They were making spitballs and paper airplanes, rather than listening as sweet Miss Nelson read during story hour. "Something will have to be done," Miss Nelson said to herself.

The next day, Miss Nelson was not at school. The children planned to misbehave worse than ever as they heard footsteps approaching the door. They were horrified to meet their substitute teacher, Miss Viola Swamp. She wore an ugly black dress and spoke in a nasty voice. The students were afraid and did exactly as they were told.

After a few days, the children missed Miss Nelson. They were beginning to think they would be stuck with Miss Swamp forever. Then one morning they heard footsteps approaching their door, and they were pleasantly surprised to find Miss Nelson approaching! During story hour that day, no one misbehaved. There were no more spitballs or paper airplanes.

That evening, Miss Nelson went home and giggled as she noticed the ugly black dress hanging in her closet.

Which of these conclusions can you make based on the clues in the story? Write **yes** or **no** next to each sentence.

_____ 1. Miss Nelson was sick.

_____ 2. Miss Nelson is a kind teacher.

_____ 3. Miss Swamp is really Miss Nelson.

_____ 4. Miss Swamp has a sister.

_____ 5. The kids in Miss Nelson's class are well behaved now.

_____ 6. The students in Miss Nelson's class miss Miss Swamp.

_____ 7. Miss Nelson will never miss school again.

Name

# Locating similarities and differences

Part of reading carefully is watching for ways that things are alike (**similarities**) and ways that they are different (**differences**).

Each of the items below are probably familiar to you. Imagine that you are comparing them to a friend who cannot see them. How are the two items alike? How are they different? Write one similarity and one difference for each.

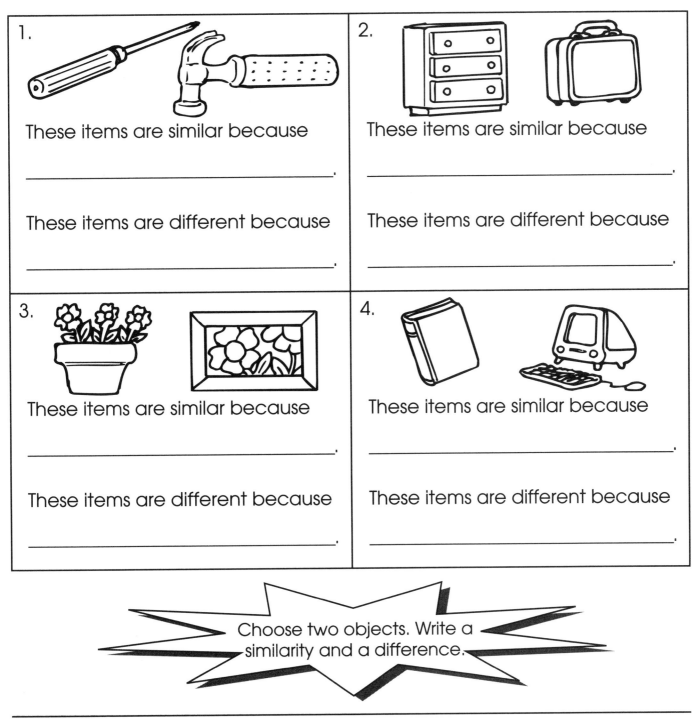

1.

These items are similar because

_____.

These items are different because

_____.

2.

These items are similar because

_____.

These items are different because

_____.

3.

These items are similar because

_____.

These items are different because

_____.

4.

These items are similar because

_____.

These items are different because

_____.

Choose two objects. Write a similarity and a difference.

## Researching for similarities and differences

Unit 5

As you read, you will notice similarities and differences that will help you draw conclusions or make decisions.

# Now or Then

Have you ever been in a convertible car? If you had lived long ago when Henry Ford starting making cars, you may have owned a convertible. He built the first cars that were low enough in price for many people to buy them. They could not go as fast as we drive today, but they looked like a lot of fun!

Ford's cars were a little different from the cars that you see today. The cars did use gas, but the tank was under the driver's seat, so you would have to lift the seat out to put gas in the car. Sometimes the cars would not start in cold weather unless you poured hot water under the hood. Many of the cars did not have bumpers or mirrors because they cost extra money. Still they were a great way to get around, just as our cars are today.

Would you rather have a car from the past or a car from today? Make a list of similarities and differences to help you decide.

How Cars of the Past and Cars of Today Are Alike

1. _____

2. _____

3. _____

How They Are Different

1. _____

2. _____

3. _____

Name

Read or listen to the directions. Fill in the circle beside the best answer.

☐ Example:

What is the best conclusion?

Bobbi grabbed a bagel from the refrigerator, threw her backpack over her shoulder, and ran for the bus.

Reread the paragraphs if you cannot remember an answer.

(A) Bobbi is running late for school.

(B) Bobbi is mad at someone.

(C) Bobbi has not eaten dinner yet.

(D) Bobbi's best friend is waiting for her on the bus.

Answer: A because Bobbi's actions tell us she is rushed.

Now try these. You have 25 minutes. Continue until you see ⬡STOP.

---

Read the story to answer questions 1–5.

### Rainbow Crow: A Lenape Tale

Long ago, before there was man, the crow was the most beautiful bird in the world. His wings were made of rainbow feathers, and his voice was the sweetest ever heard. The crow lived happily with his forest friends for many years.

Then one day, snow came to the forest for the first time ever. The animals thought little of it at first, but soon Mouse was completely buried. They knew they must stop the snow before it covered everyone. Rainbow Crow offered to fly to the Great Sky Spirit and ask him to stop the snow.

Rainbow Crow flew high toward the spirits for three days. At last, he reached the Great Sky Spirit and asked him to stop the snow. The Great One said that he could not grant his request because the snow had its own spirit. He offered to give Rainbow Crow the gift of fire to warm the earth instead. He gave the bird a flaming stick to carry in his mouth all the way back to the forest.

GO ON

Rainbow Crow flew quickly toward Earth. On the first day, he could feel sparks from the flame burning his tail feathers, but he bravely flew on. The next day Rainbow Crow noticed his wing feathers were covered with black soot from the stick's fire. On the third day of flying, Rainbow Crow could barely breathe from the fire burning his throat, but he reached the woods just in time. His friends were completely buried now, so Rainbow Crow used the flame to melt the snow. The animals were thankful and sang a beautiful song to their friend.

When the woods were quiet again, Rainbow Crow looked at himself. He was no longer beautiful, and his voice had become cracked and raspy. Crow began to cry. The Great Sky Spirit appeared to him. He explained that one day man would come to Earth and hunt animals. The Great Sky Spirit gave Crow the gift of freedom. "Man will not want your meat or your plain black feathers," he said. "But you will always know your true beauty. Look closely at your feathers, for you will see all the colors of the rainbow reflecting in them."

Crow returned to his friends in the forest, feeling proud, brave, and beautiful.

1. Which of these does not describe Rainbow Crow at the beginning of the story?

 brave
(A)

 colorful
(B)

 kind
(C)

 selfish
(D)

2. From this story, you can tell that

(A) the woodland animals were used to snow.

(B) the Great Sky Spirit lived close to the forest.

(C) the animals were afraid of fire.

(D) the crow cared about his forest friends.

GO ON

**3.** From the story, you can conclude that

(A) the Great Sky Spirit was a wise ruler.

(B) the Great Sky Spirit did not like snow.

(C) the Great Sky Spirit was evil.

(D) the Great Sky Spirit was scary.

**4.** If this story is teaching a lesson, it would be

(A) help your friends when you can.

(B) sometimes the greatest gifts are hard to see.

(C) always be the most beautiful.

(D) some beauty is hard to see at first.

**5.** How is the crow at the end of the story similar to Rainbow Crow?

(A) It feels brave and beautiful.

(B) It feels angry at the Great Sky Spirit.

(C) It has a sweet voice.

(D) It no longer lives on Earth.

Use the poem to draw conclusions for questions 6 and 7.

**Advice from My Father** by Lisa Molengraft

Each day of my childhood
My father dressed for work.
Then he joined us for breakfast,
And with a funny smirk
My father said, "Today be happy.
Be kind and yet firm.
Be the first to start your work
For the early bird catches the worm."

GO ON

**6.** What does it mean to be an early bird?

  (A) Someone who is always late.

  (B) Someone who likes birds.

  (C) Someone who is always early.

  (D) Someone who finds worms.

**7.** The author's father wanted his child to

  (A) work hard.

  (B) catch worms before school.

  (C) finish her breakfast.

  (D) make other people happy.

Read the passage to answer questions 8–10.

## Booker T. Washington

Booker T. Washington was born in Virginia in 1856 to a slave mother, making him a slave at birth. His family lived in a one-room shack that had a dirt floor and holes in the walls where animals crawled in and out. Booker's mother, Jane, worked as a cook for the family who owned the farm, or plantation. Sometimes she was able to feed her children some leftover chicken, but mostly they lived on boiled corn, roasted potatoes, and milk.

When Booker was nine years old, all the slaves were freed by the government. This gave Booker's family a chance to make their own decisions. Soon they moved to West Virginia, where Booker's interest in education began. He taught himself as much as he could through borrowed books. He was even able to attend school for a short time. Then Booker took a job that would change his life. He began cleaning house for a wealthy, extremely particular woman who made him work hard, but let him attend school in the afternoons.

GO ON

When Booker was 16, he set out for Hampton Institute in eastern Virginia. He had no money to pay for school, but he was determined to get in somehow. Booker proved himself to be such a hard worker that the school accepted him. He was a model student and finished with flying colors.

Booker T. Washington eventually started a new school, Tuskegee Institute, where he could offer other eager children a chance to learn. The school taught all subject areas, but it especially taught Booker's belief that nothing is worth having if you have not worked for it.

**8.** From the passage, you can conclude that:

(A) Many slaves went to school after they were freed.

(B) Booker was never willing to give up.

(C) Booker did not like living in Virginia.

(D) Booker taught himself how to read and write.

**9.** What does it mean to "finish with flying colors?"

(A) Booker got to hold the flag at graduation.

(B) Booker was a great art student.

(C) Booker was well-liked.

(D) Booker did a very good job.

**10.** How was Booker's life different after his family was freed?

(A) They lived in a nice house in Virginia.

(B) They had better meals to eat.

(C) They could make decisions for themselves.

(D) They had more money.

For 11–14, match each sentence below with its logical conclusion.

A. The Midwestern part of the U.S. was unprepared for its September snowstorm.

B. The teachers and students are working hard to help save Earth.

C. The number of students at Greenway School is growing.

D. The summer heat has been tough on flowers and plants.

**11.** The recycling bin at our school is overflowing.

Ⓐ      Ⓑ      Ⓒ      Ⓓ

**12.** We will be replacing the lilac bushes in front of our house.

Ⓐ      Ⓑ      Ⓒ      Ⓓ

**13.** The squirrels had few nuts stored for winter.

Ⓐ      Ⓑ      Ⓒ      Ⓓ

**14.** The construction team is adding four additional classrooms.

Ⓐ      Ⓑ      Ⓒ      Ⓓ

**15.** Using the information given, which sentence does not seem like a logical inference?

The parking lot at the movie theater was packed.

Ⓐ Many people have come to the theater.

Ⓑ The movie they are showing is popular.

Ⓒ The theater will probably be crowded.

Ⓓ The movie will be your favorite.

GO ON ▷

# Unit 5 Test

**16.** Which of these items is similar to a football field in length?

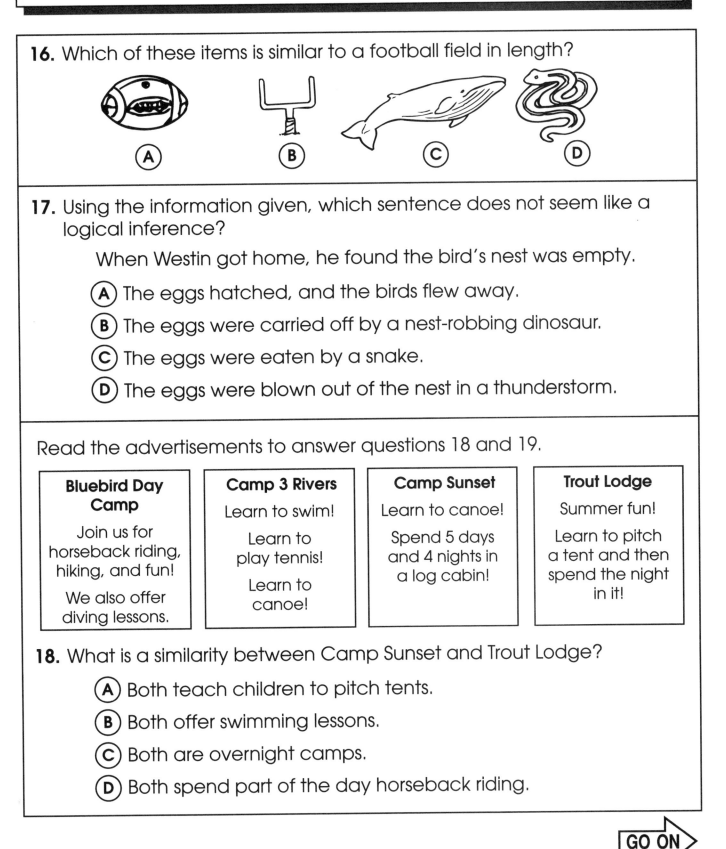

Ⓐ     Ⓑ     Ⓒ     Ⓓ

**17.** Using the information given, which sentence does not seem like a logical inference?

When Westin got home, he found the bird's nest was empty.

Ⓐ The eggs hatched, and the birds flew away.

Ⓑ The eggs were carried off by a nest-robbing dinosaur.

Ⓒ The eggs were eaten by a snake.

Ⓓ The eggs were blown out of the nest in a thunderstorm.

Read the advertisements to answer questions 18 and 19.

| **Bluebird Day Camp** | **Camp 3 Rivers** | **Camp Sunset** | **Trout Lodge** |
|---|---|---|---|
| Join us for horseback riding, hiking, and fun! We also offer diving lessons. | Learn to swim! Learn to play tennis! Learn to canoe! | Learn to canoe! Spend 5 days and 4 nights in a log cabin! | Summer fun! Learn to pitch a tent and then spend the night in it! |

**18.** What is a similarity between Camp Sunset and Trout Lodge?

Ⓐ Both teach children to pitch tents.

Ⓑ Both offer swimming lessons.

Ⓒ Both are overnight camps.

Ⓓ Both spend part of the day horseback riding.

GO ON ▷

**19.** Samantha is an excellent swimmer, but she would like to learn to dive. Next month, she will be visiting her aunt who raises horses, and she has no interest in tennis. Which camp do you think Samantha will choose?

(A) Bluebird Day Camp

(B) Camp Sunset

(C) Trout Lodge

(D) Camp 3 Rivers

**20.** Which object is similar to a fork because of its shape?

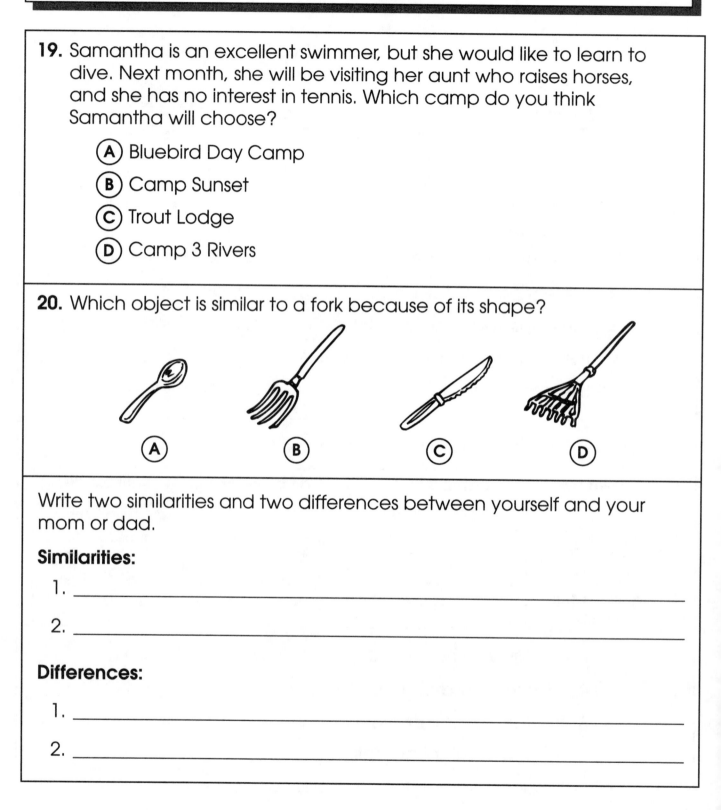

(A)          (B)          (C)          (D)

Write two similarities and two differences between yourself and your mom or dad.

**Similarities:**

1. _____

2. _____

**Differences:**

1. _____

2. _____

Name

## Fact vs. opinion

**Facts** are real and true statements. **Opinions** are ideas, feelings, or beliefs.

Read each sentence and mark it as a fact or an opinion. Then write your own four sentences and ask a friend or family member to label them as facts or opinions.

|  | Fact | Opinion |
|---|---|---|
| 1. The temperature is 82° F. | | |
| 2. Gina's sister is really cute. | | |
| 3. <u>Harry Potter</u> was a better book than a movie. | | |
| 4. Jack did a better job on the test than I did. | | |
| 5. This year's carnival was more fun than last year's. | | |
| 6. It took us eight and a half hours to get to Akron. | | |
| 7. Philadelphia got six inches of snow yesterday. | | |
| 8. It is too cold to play outside. | | |
| 9. Asparagus tastes awful. | | |
| 10. Football is the toughest sport. | | |
| 11. Blue whales can be up to 100 feet long. | | |
| 12. Geometry is easy. | | |
| 13. Maple and oak trees grow well in the Midwest. | | |
| 14. | | |
| 15. | | |
| 16. | | |
| 17. | | |

# Discovering facts and opinions

Unit 6

Informational passages are written to teach you something. In them you may find facts, opinions, or a mix of both.

## Native-American Dances

Native Americans have long used dancing to express themselves. Each dance has deep and emotional meaning to the tribe. The Fancy Dance is fast and colorful with the Great Plains dancers dressed in feathers and painted masks. It is the most exciting of the dances. The Hoop Dance is performed with large hoops that the dancers keep swinging and shaping to resemble patterns from nature. It is by far the most difficult dance. The Butterfly Dance honors the animal for which it is named. The Pueblo dancers, wearing butterfly headdresses, imitate the peaceful life of this creature. The dance is graceful and beautiful.

Write three facts from the passage.

1. _____

2. _____

3. _____

Write three opinions from the passage.

1. _____

2. _____

3. _____

**80**

Name

# Classifying

**Classifying** means putting things in groups. One way to group things is to look for similarities. For example, you can group things by days, months, or years. History books are often classified by time.

The names of several American presidents are written below. Classify them by the years they began their terms as president.

| 1901 | T. Roosevelt | 1974 | G. Ford | 1945 | H. Truman |
|------|-------------|------|---------|------|-----------|
| 1885 | G. Cleveland | 2001 | G. W. Bush | 1817 | J. Monroe |
| 1993 | B. Clinton | 1789 | G. Washington | 1861 | A. Lincoln |
| 1797 | J. Adams | 1845 | J. Polk | 1801 | T. Jefferson |
| 1837 | M. Van Buren | 1869 | U. Grant | 1981 | R. Reagan |
| 1913 | W. Wilson | 1961 | J. Kennedy | 1929 | H. Hoover |

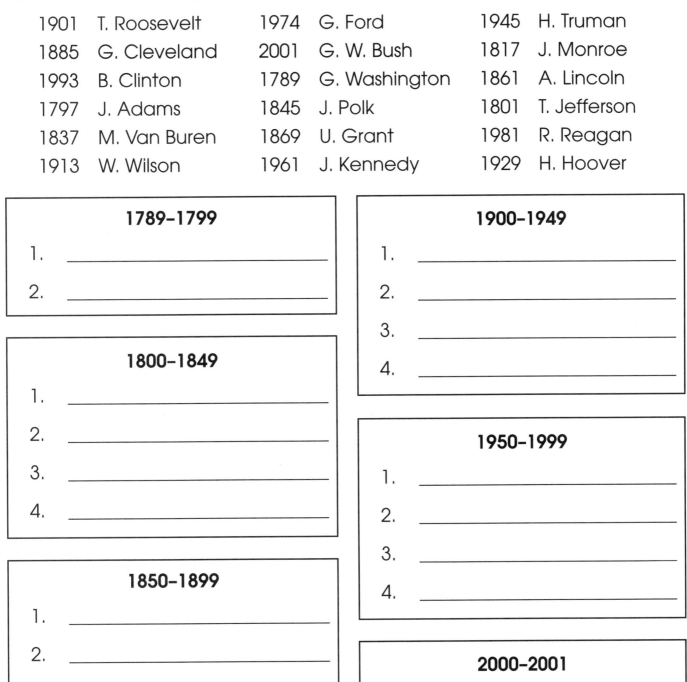

**1789–1799**

1. _____
2. _____

**1800–1849**

1. _____
2. _____
3. _____
4. _____

**1850–1899**

1. _____
2. _____
3. _____

**1900–1949**

1. _____
2. _____
3. _____
4. _____

**1950–1999**

1. _____
2. _____
3. _____
4. _____

**2000–2001**

1. _____

Name

## Classifying by characteristics

Unit 6

When you are looking for the item that does not belong in a group, try to find the one thing the others have in common. Example: star, moon, rocket, planet
The rocket does not fit because it is not a natural part of the solar system.

Cross out the word that does not belong with the others.

| 1. | 2. | 3. | 4. |
|---|---|---|---|
| boot | Little Dipper | paper clip | celery |
| sandal | Orion the Hunter | gum | lettuce |
| sock | Big Dipper | tape | apple |
| slipper | Uranus | syrup | broccoli |

| 5. | 6. | 7. | 8. |
|---|---|---|---|
| sailfish | pink | candle | heart |
| tuna | yellow | mirror | green |
| swordfish | blue | flashlight | leprechaun |
| dolphin | red | lantern | clover |

| 9. | 10. | 11. | 12. |
|---|---|---|---|
| ears | stairs | purse | George Bush |
| eyes | vacuum | pocket | Ben Franklin |
| nose | mountain | nest | Abe Lincoln |
| eyebrows | ladder | window | John Adams |

Write the names of 12 items that are in your closet. Then classify them into groups.

## Predicting a story's outcome

There are often clues hidden in a story that give you an idea of what will happen next.

Mark an **X** by the sentence that tells what will probably happen next.

### No More Help!

Lulu and her mother were excited to spend the morning at the park with her three-year-old twin brothers, Mickey and Jonathan. Lulu offered to start packing their lunches while her mom dressed the boys. It was not long before Mickey appeared at Lulu's feet asking to help. Lulu explained that she was in a hurry to get to the park. Mickey turned to the refrigerator and took out the grapes, trying to help. The bowl was much too big for him to hold, and . . .

1. _____ Mickey put the grapes in the lunch basket.

_____ Mickey dropped the bowl.

_____ Mickey ate all of the grapes.

Grapes went everywhere. At that moment, Jonathan came running into the room and slid on the grapes. Lulu grabbed the broom while her mom settled the boys in the other room. As Lulu and her mom finished the floor, they heard a loud crash in the broom closet. Mickey and Jonathan were standing there with the vacuum in their hands. Apparently they wanted to help clean up the grapes but the vacuum had fallen, breaking the dust bag open. The boys were . . .

2. _____ sitting in a pile of dust.

_____ playing with their blocks.

_____ laughing at a movie.

Lulu and her mother quickly cleaned them up and headed for the car. "Oh, no," Mom said. "I forgot to feed the dog." Hearing this, . . .

3. _____ Mickey and Jonathan jumped into their car seats.

_____ Mickey and Jonathan asked for a snack.

_____ Mickey and Jonathan ran toward the big bag of dog food.

"We help," they shouted. Mom laughed and said, . . .

4. _____ "Okay, you can fill the water bowl."

_____ "I think you've already helped enough today."

_____ "Great. Lulu and I will wait in the car."

Name

## Making your own predictions

Use the clues from the story to predict what will happen next.

Make your predictions as you come to the questions. Do not read ahead!

### The Bremen-Town Musicians

A long time ago there lived an old donkey who had faithfully served his master for many years. The donkey had since become too old to carry sacks of grain, and his master planned to do away with him. The donkey developed a plan to run away to the town of Bremen where he would become a musician. The donkey had not gone too far when he came upon an old hunting dog lying in the road. The dog explained that he had become too old to hunt any longer, and that his master had plans to do away with him.

1. What do you think will happen next? _____

_____

2. What makes you think so?_____

_____

The donkey suggested that the dog join him in Bremen to become a musician. The dog agreed, and the two of them continued their journey. Farther down the road, the friends happened upon an old cat and an old rooster, both fearing for their lives as well. They decided to join the donkey and the dog. As night fell, the four travelers became tired and hungry. They spotted a house in the woods and approached it. Peering in, they found a table full of food and a band of robbers sitting around it. The four friends screeched out their music as loud as they could, scaring the robbers away.

3. What will the four musicians do now? _____

_____

4. What makes you think so?_____

_____

After the animals had fallen asleep, the robbers came back to the house. They saw the cat's eyes reflecting light and began to run. The dog bit their legs, the donkey kicked them, and the rooster crowed. The robbers were so scared they never returned to the house again.

5. What will the animals do now? _____

Name

Read or listen to the directions. Fill in the circle beside the best answer.

☐ Example:

Jason heard the trash truck coming and remembered his job wasn't done yet.

What will probably happen next in the story?

(A) Jason ran toward the garage and quickly wheeled the trash cans outside.

(B) Jason waved to the trash man.

(C) Jason went back to reading his book.

(D) Jason went downstairs to finish the dishes.

More than one answer may seem correct! Be sure to compare the choices.

Answer: A because the trash truck reminded Jason of his job, taking out the trash.

Now try these. You have 25 minutes. Continue until you see ⬡STOP .

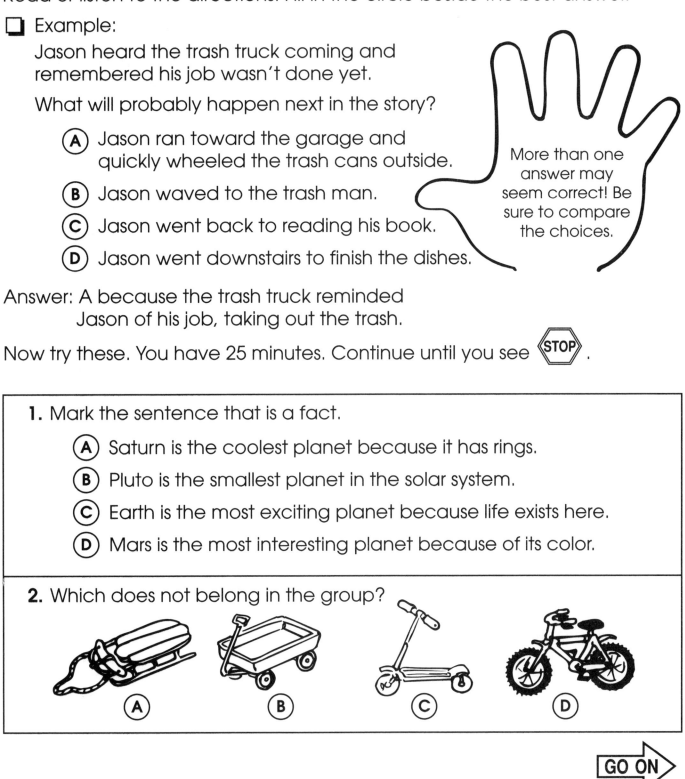

1. Mark the sentence that is a fact.

(A) Saturn is the coolest planet because it has rings.

(B) Pluto is the smallest planet in the solar system.

(C) Earth is the most exciting planet because life exists here.

(D) Mars is the most interesting planet because of its color.

2. Which does not belong in the group?

(A)      (B)      (C)      (D)

GO ON ▷

**3.** Mark the sentence that is an opinion.

(A) It's a law in many states that small children must be in car seats.

(B) Wearing a seat belt can help save lives in an accident.

(C) Everyone should wear a seat belt.

(D) Some new cars are made with car seats built into them.

**4.** Hans packed his suitcase. He put gloves, a wool hat, and heavy boots inside. Where will Hans go?

(A) to the beach

(B) to school

(C) to his cousin's house

(D) to the mountains

Read the letter to answer questions 5–8.

Dear Mr. and Mrs. Jones,

The new school year is just around the corner, and we want your child to be prepared. Below you will find a list of supplies that Alexa needs to bring with her on August 28, the first day of school. Be sure to label each of them with Alexa's name.

| | |
|---|---|
| 8 pencils | 3 glue sticks |
| 4 spiral notebooks | 1 pair of scissors |
| 2 packages of colored pencils | 2 packages of markers |
| 1 box of tissue | 1 school box |

I cannot wait to meet everyone. I am really excited to be the new principal at Baker Elementary. This is going to the best year ever!

Thank you,

Mrs. Barnes

**5.** Which of the supplies seems different from the others?

(A) 8 pencils

(B) 2 packages of markers

(C) 1 pair of scissors

(D) 1 box of tissues

GO ON

**6.** Which is an opinion from the letter?

(A) This is going to be the best year ever.

(B) The first day of school is August 28.

(C) Ms. Barnes wants the students to be prepared.

(D) Alexa needs to bring her supplies.

**7.** What do you think Mr. and Mrs. Jones will do after they read the letter?

(A) They will probably call the school.

(B) They will probably go on vacation before August 28.

(C) They will go shopping for the supplies.

(D) They will take Alexa to the amusement park before school starts.

**8.** Which is not a fact from the letter?

(A) The school has a new principal this year.

(B) Alexa is going to be in the third grade.

(C) Alexa goes to an elementary school.

(D) Alexa's name should be on her supplies.

**9.** Which is an opinion?

(A) The Olympic Games are the toughest games in the world.

(B) The Olympic Games started in Greece.

(C) The Olympic sprinters can run more than 20 miles per hour.

(D) Only men were allowed to enter the first Olympic Games.

GO ON

Read the story to answer questions 10–12.

Tobi was furious! He got home from school and found that his baseball cards were scattered all over his room. Just then, his four-year-old brother, Tyler, came in. "Hi Tobi! I wanted to find your lost football card for you and guess what? I did find it. It was mixed in with your other cards," he said. He looked so pleased with himself.

**10.** What do you think Tobi will say?

(A) "Great job!"

(B) "Thanks, but next time wait for me to get home."

(C) "You can come into my room anytime."

(D) "You're so funny, Tyler."

**11.** Which of these may be the missing card?

(A)          (B)          (C)          (D)

**12.** Which of these is not a fact from the story?

(A) Tobi was angry when he saw his room.

(B) Tobi was missing a card.

(C) Tobi's brother is four years old.

(D) Tyler collects baseball cards.

GO ON

Read the story to answer questions 13–15.

Jack watched his friends playing follow-the-leader off the diving board. He did not want to be left out, but he was afraid of the diving board. Later that day, Jack asked his dad to teach him how to dive. They practiced all afternoon. The next weekend, Jack packed his bag to meet his friends at the pool again.

**13.** What do you think Jack will do?

(A) He will probably stay home.

(B) He may ask his friends to play a different game.

(C) He will probably play follow-the-leader this time.

(D) He may only swim with his dad.

**14.** Which of these is a fact from the story?

(A) Jack practiced hard to learn to dive.

(B) Jack's friends were on the diving team.

(C) Jack became a good swimmer.

(D) Jack's friends could swim underwater.

**15.** Which of these would probably not be found in Jack's bag?

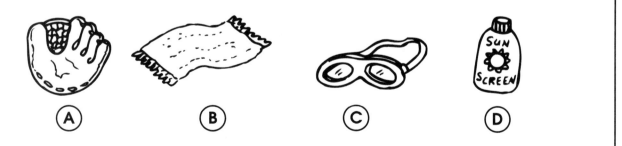

(A)          (B)          (C)          (D)

Name

**16.** Mark the sentence that tells what probably happens next.

Steve pulled back his arm, ready to throw the football to his brother. Then he remembered what happened last time they played ball in the house.

(A) Steve carefully threw the ball to his brother.

(B) Steve's brother tackled him.

(C) Steve suggested they play outside instead.

(D) Steve's mom walked in, and both boys were grounded.

Mark the word that does not belong in each group in 17–20.

| **17.** | kangaroo | fish | cat | turtle |
|---|---|---|---|---|
| | (A) | (B) | (C) | (D) |
| **18.** | noun | verb | period | adverb |
| | (A) | (B) | (C) | (D) |
| **19.** | wood | wallpaper | carpet | tile |
| | (A) | (B) | (C) | (D) |
| **20.** | angle | octagon | rectangle | square |
| | (A) | (B) | (C) | (D) |

Write two items that would be classified in the group on the left. Then write another group name and list two items.

**Two-Syllable Words**                           _____

1. _____          1. _____

2. _____          2. _____

STOP

## Analyzing characters                                          Unit 7

**Characters** are people, animals, or animated objects that are found in a story. The most important characters are called main characters. They seem to be brought to life by their actions. You may even witness a character's personality change as a story unfolds.

### In a Neighborly Way

Casey was excited to meet his new neighbors. He had watched the new family move in and could not wait to meet their son who looked about Casey's age. It did not take long for the boys to become friendly, and soon Casey asked his new neighbor, Nick, to play at his house. The boys spent the first hour playing the games that Nick chose. Casey did not mind because he knew it was polite to let the guest choose. After another half hour, Casey thought it should be his turn to choose a game.

"No, I don't want to," Nick stubbornly replied.

"But I haven't chosen a game yet," Casey said.

"Well, if you won't play what I want, I'm going home," Nick threatened.

Casey did not want his new friend to leave, so he agreed to play Nick's chosen game.

The next time Casey's mom offered to invite Nick over, Casey declined. He told his mom how selfishly Nick had acted before. His mom offered an idea.

Nick came over that afternoon, and it was not long before he threatened to leave again. This time Casey said, "Okay, you can go home. I really wanted to be friends, but I want friends who are fair. I'll see you later."

Nick could not believe his ears! Would his new friend really let him leave? He thought about the way he had acted and said, "I'm sorry. Let's play the game you choose now. I want to be a fair friend."

1. Write two adjectives to describe Casey.

   a. _____          b. _____

2. Write two adjectives to describe Nick at the beginning of the story.

   a. _____          b. _____

3. Write two adjectives to describe Nick at the end of the story.

   a. _____          b. _____

## Exploring the problem

Unit 7

Stories are more interesting when a character has to face a problem, then figure out a way to address it. Much of a story's adventure happens while a character is solving the problem.

In the story below, the main character faces three problems. Watch for them as you read.

### The Littlest Bear

The littlest bear at the North Pole was also the loneliest bear at the North Pole. He spent each day wishing for a friend his own size. Then one day he watched the older bears building snow friends. Suddenly the little bear knew how to solve his problem. He spent the entire day building a snow bear to look just like himself. He wrapped a scarf around his friend's neck and slipped boots over his feet. Then the littlest bear realized that his friend could not play inside his house. "That's okay," he thought. He ran inside, grabbed an old blanket, and collected his toys. He spread the blanket out on the snow and laid his toys on top. The two bears spent the rest of the winter playing and laughing. The little bear never felt lonely for a minute. Then the spring air came to the North Pole, melting the snow bear to the ground. At first the littlest bear was sad, but as he knelt down to the puddle, he saw his own reflection. He realized that he had grown over the winter months and was no longer the littlest bear. Even better, he was no longer the loneliest bear!

1. What was the littlest bear's first problem? _____

_____

2. How did he solve the problem? _____

_____

3. What was another of the littlest bear's problems? _____

_____

4. How did he solve it? _____

_____

Name

## Discovering the setting

The **setting** is the place and time in which a story takes place. As a story unfolds, the setting may change. The book <u>Brother Eagle, Sister Sky</u> by Susan J. Jeffers (Penguin Putnam Books for Young Readers, 1991) offers an example of this.

In the fight to save his tribe's land, Chief Seattle spoke of his desire to preserve the American land. In this book, he begs us to care for our earth as we would our brother. He also questions what will become of all men if we don't.

Draw the settings that are described.

If people use the land wisely, there will always be beautiful forests, oceans, and deserts full of living plants and animals.

If our land becomes too polluted, we will lose natural beauty. The forests, oceans, and deserts will be replaced by factories and phone wires.

**93**

Name

## Developing a story

As characters try to solve their problems, a story develops and other things begin to happen. This is called the **plot** of the story. The plot is often divided into three parts: the beginning, middle, and end.

Combine the characters, setting, and plot to plan a story of your own. Together, these elements make a story.

1. Plan two characters. Write their names and three words to describe them.

   1. _____

      1. _____

      2. _____

      3. _____

   2. _____

      1. _____

      2. _____

      3. _____

2. Describe your setting. _____

_____

_____

3. What problem will your characters face? _____

_____

_____

4. How will they solve the problem? _____

_____

_____

Name

5. How will your plot unfold? Plan the beginning, middle, and end of your story.

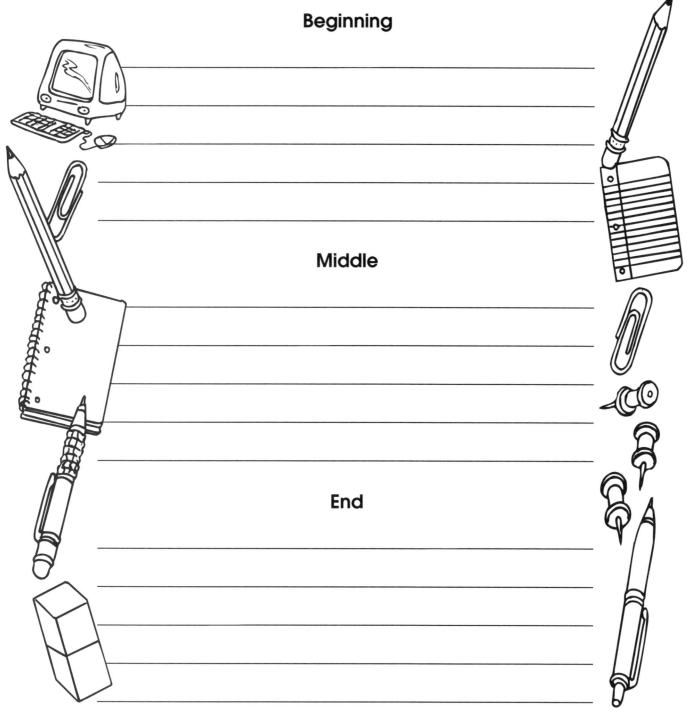

**Beginning**

**Middle**

**End**

6. Turn your plan into a story or book. Use a pencil and paper or a computer, then share your story with a friend.

Name

## Following directions

Unlike stories, **directions** have no plot. Instead, they will help the reader do something or get somewhere. Directions should be read one at a time and followed exactly. It may be easy to lose your place or skip important parts. To prevent this, be sure to check the directions off as you complete them.

Use the chart to follow the course of two airplanes as they carry travelers around the United States. Use a red marker to show the path of the Air America plane. Use a blue marker to show the path of the Nations Air plane.

|  | Took off from | 1st Stop | 2nd Stop | 3rd Stop | 4th Stop | 5th Stop | Final Stop |
|---|---|---|---|---|---|---|---|
| **Air America** | Utah (UT) | Colorado (CO) | Texas (TX) | Louisiana (LA) | Tennessee (TN) | Virginia (VA) | Florida (FL) |
| **Nations Air** | Michigan (MI) | New York (NY) | Maryland (MD) | Georgia (GA) | Louisiana (LA) | Kansas (KS) | Arizona (AZ) |

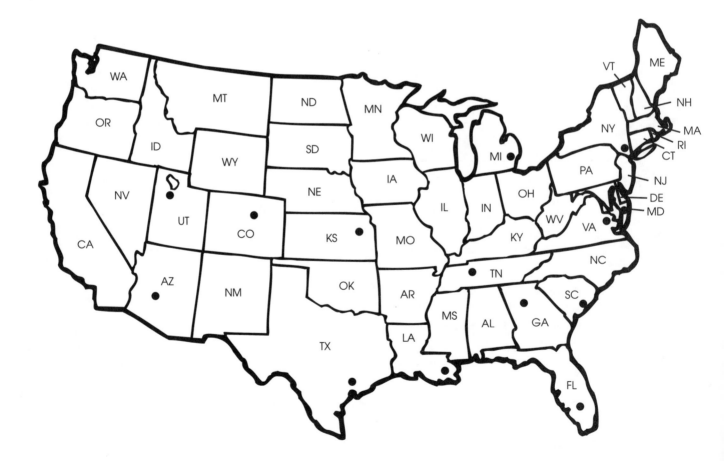

Name

Read or listen to the directions. Fill in the circle beside the best answer.

□ Example:

Jonna threw herself on her bed and buried her head in her pillow.

How do you think Jonna is feeling?

(A) proud        (B) discouraged

(C) pleased      (D) clever

Answer: B because the character's actions describe her feelings.

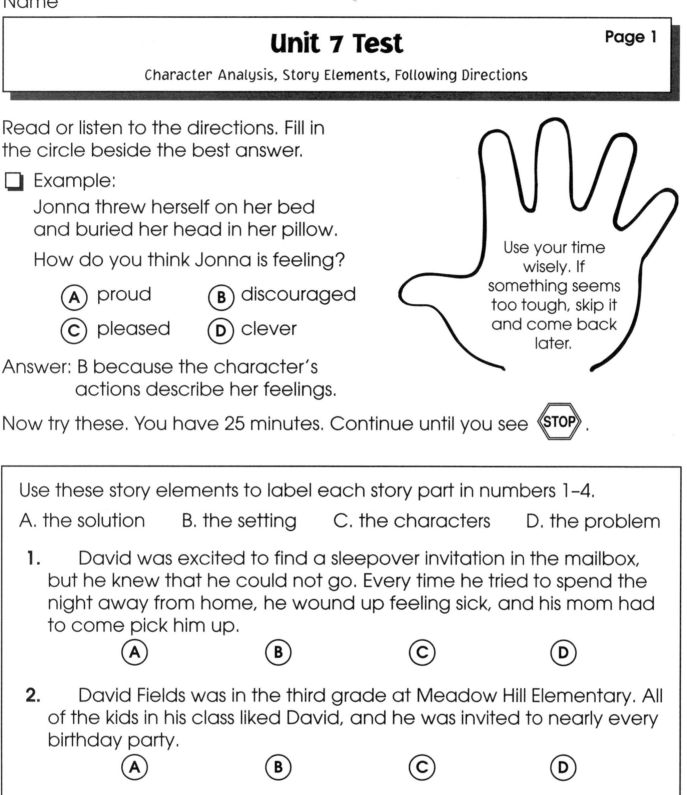

Use your time wisely. If something seems too tough, skip it and come back later.

Now try these. You have 25 minutes. Continue until you see ⬡STOP .

---

Use these story elements to label each story part in numbers 1–4.

A. the solution      B. the setting      C. the characters      D. the problem

1.    David was excited to find a sleepover invitation in the mailbox, but he knew that he could not go. Every time he tried to spend the night away from home, he wound up feeling sick, and his mom had to come pick him up.

(A)            (B)            (C)            (D)

2.    David Fields was in the third grade at Meadow Hill Elementary. All of the kids in his class liked David, and he was invited to nearly every birthday party.

(A)            (B)            (C)            (D)

---

GO ON ▷

**3.** David's dad had an idea. He helped David pack his bag for the sleepover. At the bottom, in a secret spot, David's dad put a picture of their family and David's favorite stuffed animal. "Now you will feel like the whole family is sleeping over," he told David.

(A)     (B)     (C)     (D)

**4.** The boys slept in the basement for the sleepover. There was a big screen TV, a pool table, and a pinball machine.

(A)     (B)     (C)     (D)

**5.** Which of these would not be used to describe a character's feelings?

astonished     confused     teach     nervous
(A)              (B)          (C)       (D)

Read the story to answer questions 6–9.

### The Science Project

Ms. Henry had insisted that every student enter the science fair this year. Kyle was assigned to Seth as a partner, much to Kyle's disappointment. Everyone knew that Seth was the laziest kid in the class. He never finished his assignments, and he was always doodling rather than listening. The boys decided to meet at Kyle's house after school to plan their project.

Seth arrived with a backpack bursting with test tubes, magnets, crystals, and every type of science experiment equipment you could imagine. Kyle was surprised. Why would this lazy kid have such cool stuff? When Kyle suggested building a model of the solar system, Seth pulled out painted foam balls and rattled off all types of facts about each model planet. Kyle was surprised again. Maybe Kyle had been mistaken about Seth.

At last, the boys agreed to experiment to find the best place to store bananas. Seth had an idea of what the answer would be, but he had never truly performed the experiment. The boys met each day after school and

were confident that their experiment would be the best. Kyle worked on writing the report, while Seth continued to question and experiment further. They found they made quite a team.

At the Science Center on the day of the judging, Ms. Henry told Kyle that she was proud of him for helping Seth with the project. Kyle had to explain that Seth was responsible for much of the work. He went on to ask if Seth could be his partner for next month's math project.

**6.** Which of these does not describe Seth's work on the project?

helpful      lazy      smart      curious

Ⓐ      Ⓑ      Ⓒ      Ⓓ

**7.** What does the reader learn about Seth?

Ⓐ He is smart and probably doodles because he is bored.

Ⓑ He is lazy and will never win the science fair.

Ⓒ He will probably never do well in school.

Ⓓ He is one of Ms. Henry's best students.

**8.** Which is not a setting in this story?

Ⓐ Kyle's house      Ⓑ school

Ⓒ the Science Center      Ⓓ Seth's house

**9.** Which part of the plot happened in the beginning of the story?

Ⓐ Kyle was disappointed to have Seth as a partner.

Ⓑ Ms. Henry thanked Kyle for helping Seth.

Ⓒ The boys realized they made a good team.

Ⓓ Kyle began to realize that Seth was pretty smart.

GO ON

Read the story to answer questions 10–14.

## The Daredevil

J.J. had always loved adventure. But no matter how many times he was warned about safety, J.J. never paid attention. He had broken his arm twice and his ankle once, but still thought he could do anything, no matter the danger involved. Last winter, J.J. wanted to practice ice skating. His mother had warned him many times not to skate on the pond alone. There would be no one to help him if he had an accident. J.J. tried to find a friend to join him, but all of his friends were busy. He strapped on his skates and headed out on the ice. He practiced his speed and his turns. As he was gaining speed, he heard the ice crack a couple of times but thought nothing of it.

Then it happened. In an instant, the ice under J.J.'s skates gave way, and he found himself falling under the icy water. Instinctively, J.J. grabbed onto the sheet of ice as his head went under water. He quickly pulled himself back out and grabbed a breath of air. As he struggled to pull himself out of the water, the ice continued to break away. He could not get out! He was scared and tired of struggling when he saw his dad running toward him with a rope. J.J. grabbed hold of the rope, and his dad pulled him to safety. J.J.'s eyes were full of tears as he held his dad tight. Now he understood that danger is very real.

**10.** Which of these describes J.J. at the beginning of the story?

careful
(A)

scared
(B)

cautious
(C)

dangerous
(D)

**11.** How do you think J.J. will act now?

(A) He will probably take more chances.

(B) He may be more careful.

(C) He may ice skate alone more often.

(D) He will probably be a better skater.

GO ON

**12.** What could the reader assume about J.J.'s broken arm and ankle?

(A) J.J. probably broke them by falling down the steps.

(B) J.J. may have broken them when he was swimming.

(C) J.J. probably broke them doing something dangerous.

(D) J.J. may have broken them when he was learning to walk.

**13.** Which part of the plot happened in the middle of the story?

(A) J.J. broke his ankle.    (B) J.J. fell through the ice.

(C) J.J. broke his arm.    (D) J.J.'s dad pulled him to safety.

**14.** Which of these is not a problem in the story?

(A) J.J. takes dangerous chances.    (B) J.J. broke his arm.

(C) J.J. went skating alone.    (D) J.J. does not follow rules.

**15.** Mark the drawing of the student who followed the directions.

Draw a striped circle in a black box next to a polka-dotted triangle.

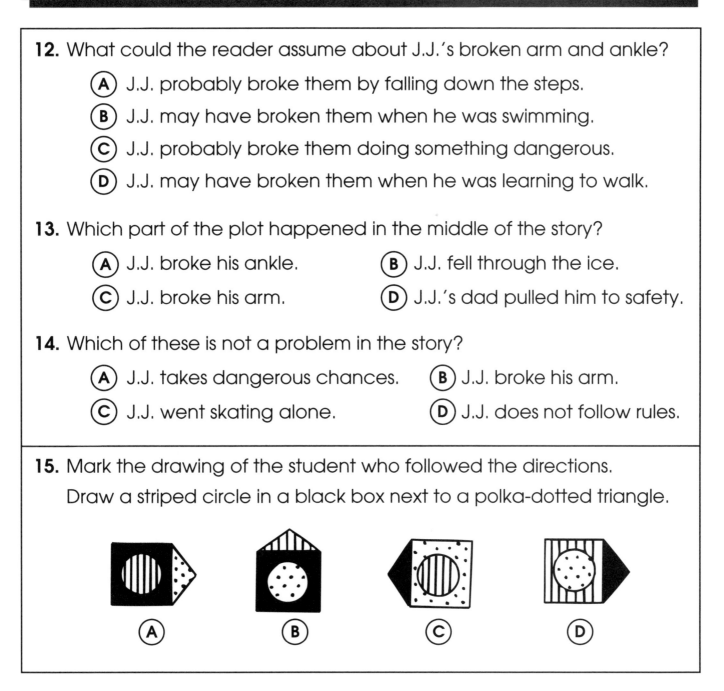

(A)          (B)          (C)          (D)

**16.** Which of these adjectives describes a setting?

   (A) soft          (B) furry

   (C) sunny         (D) angry

**17.** Which of these might an observant character say?

   (A) "I do not like roast beef sandwiches."

   (B) "I finally taught my dog, Doc, to shake hands."

   (C) "The phone is for Mom."

   (D) "Didn't you wear that sweater yesterday?"

For questions 18–20, match each picture with its directions.

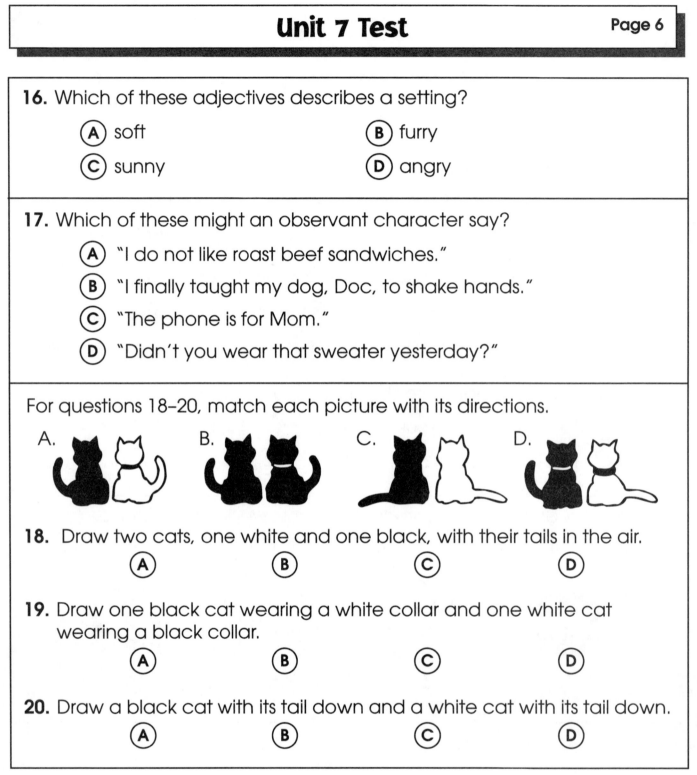

A.          B.          C.          D.

**18.** Draw two cats, one white and one black, with their tails in the air.

   (A)          (B)          (C)          (D)

**19.** Draw one black cat wearing a white collar and one white cat wearing a black collar.

   (A)          (B)          (C)          (D)

**20.** Draw a black cat with its tail down and a white cat with its tail down.

   (A)          (B)          (C)          (D)

GO ON

Name

Write a set of directions explaining how to do one of these activities: playing a movie in a VCR, making a turkey sandwich, or getting from your house to your friend's house.

_____

_____

_____

_____

_____

_____

_____

_____

_____

_____

_____

_____

Name

## Using an encyclopedia                                        Unit 8

An **encyclopedia** is a book or a set of books containing informative, factual information. On the outside of each book or volume, is a letter or letters that show what topics can be found inside each book. Within the volumes, everything is alphabetized (by last name if a person).

Write the volume number that would help you find each answer.

_____ 1. Who was the eleventh president?

_____ 2. Who was Babe Ruth?

_____ 3. Where is the capital of Argentina?

_____ 4. Where is the Red Sea located?

_____ 5. When did Hawaii become a state?

_____ 6. What does an anaconda eat?

_____ 7. Who was involved in World War I?

_____ 8. Who invented the television?

List four subjects that would be found in the F volume from a set of encyclopedias.

# Using a card catalog

The **card catalog** helps you learn more about a book without actually seeing the book.

**Title:** Charlotte's Web

**Author:** White, E.B.: illustrated by Garth Williams

**Published:** New York; Harper and Row Publishers, Inc., ©1952

**Physical Description:** 184 p.

**Summary:** Wilbur was lovingly raised by a girl named Fern. But now he is a barn pig. He is bored and lonely—until he meets Charlotte, the beautiful gray spider who also lives in the barn. Charlotte thinks of a way to save Wilbur from a pig's unhappy fate.

**Notes:** Interest grade level: 3–6

**Subject:** Adventure Fiction

Use your favorite book to create your own card for a card catalog.

**Title:** _____

**Author:** _____

**Published:** _____

**Physical Description:** _____

**Summary:** _____

_____

_____

**Notes:** _____

**Subject:** _____

Name

## Choosing reference materials

Who was our third president? How high is Mount Everest? What will the weather be like tomorrow? To find the answers to such questions, you may look in any of these places:

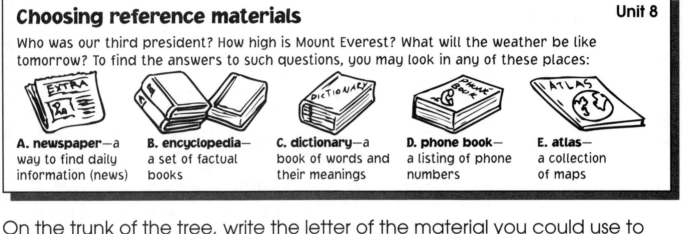

**A. newspaper**—a way to find daily information (news)

**B. encyclopedia**—a set of factual books

**C. dictionary**—a book of words and their meanings

**D. phone book**—a listing of phone numbers

**E. atlas**—a collection of maps

On the trunk of the tree, write the letter of the material you could use to find the answer.

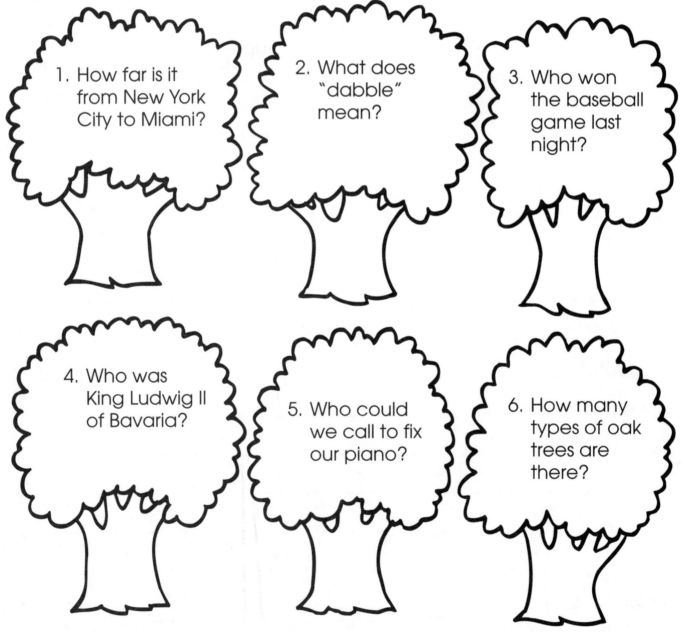

1. How far is it from New York City to Miami?

2. What does "dabble" mean?

3. Who won the baseball game last night?

4. Who was King Ludwig II of Bavaria?

5. Who could we call to fix our piano?

6. How many types of oak trees are there?

Name

## Reading a chart
<blockquote>

Unit 8

**Charts** and **tables** are helpful in organizing information. To read a chart, match your given information from the top and side to find new information in the boxes.

Example: What assignment is due in math on Tuesday?

Find the subject, math, along the side and follow it to Tuesday. You will find pages 23–24 in the space.
</blockquote>

| Subjects | Monday | Tuesday | Wednesday | Thursday | Friday |
|---|---|---|---|---|---|
| **Reading** | unit 1 | unit 2 | unit 3 | unit 4 | review |
| **Writing** | brainstorm | rough draft | revise | edit | final draft |
| **Math** | p. 21–22 | p. 23–24 | p. 25–26 | p. 27–30 | line graph |
| **Science** | plant seeds | | record | | record |
| **S. Studies** | | finish map | | time line | |

Use the information from the chart to find the answers.

1. What assignment is due on Wednesday in science? _____

2. What assignment is due on Thursday in writing? _____

3. On what day is the time line due in social studies? _____

4. In what subject do we read pages 27–30 on Thursday? _____

5. What assignment is due on Monday in social studies? _____

6. On what day is unit 2 due in reading? _____

7. On what day is the line graph due in math? _____

8. What assignment is due Tuesday in writing? _____

Name

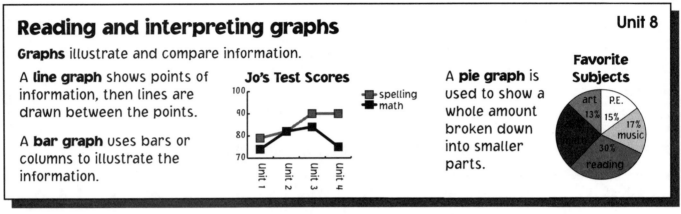

## Reading and interpreting graphs

**Graphs** illustrate and compare information.

A **line graph** shows points of information, then lines are drawn between the points.

A **bar graph** uses bars or columns to illustrate the information.

A **pie graph** is used to show a whole amount broken down into smaller parts.

Use the information from the bar graph to answer each question.

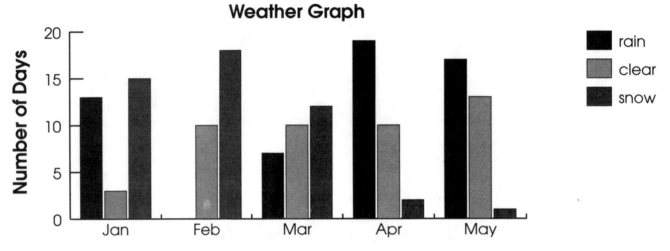

1. Patsy just bought a new pair of snow boots. In which month will Patsy probably wear them the most? _____

2. Based on the graph, when is the best time to plant new water-loving grass? _____

3. Which type of weather would you predict will occur for the least number of days in June? _____

4. The snack bar noticed they sold more hot chocolate during certain months. Based on the graph, which months would you predict they were? _____ and _____

5. In which two months are the weather patterns most similar?
_____ and _____

## Analyzing words through analogies

**Analogies** are one way to compare and analyze words. The best way to solve an analogy is to look only at the first two words. How are they related to one another? Now apply that same relationship to the next set of words.

Example: Fish is to water as camel is to _____. Fish is related to water because it is its habitat. What is the habitat of a camel? The answer is desert.

Who will win the game of tic-tac-toe? Finish each analogy using words from the game board. Then mark an **X** or **O** over the words on the board to find the winner!

1. Circle is to sphere as square is to _____. Mark X.

2. Yellow is to flame as orange is to _____. Mark O.

3. Food is to pantry as clothes is to _____. Mark X.

4. Two is to pair as twelve is to _____. Mark O.

5. Limb is to tree as leg is to _____. Mark X.

6. Corner is to square as point is to _____. Mark O.

7. Bucket is to pail as path is to _____. Mark X.

8. Shovel is to dig as broom is to _____. Mark O.

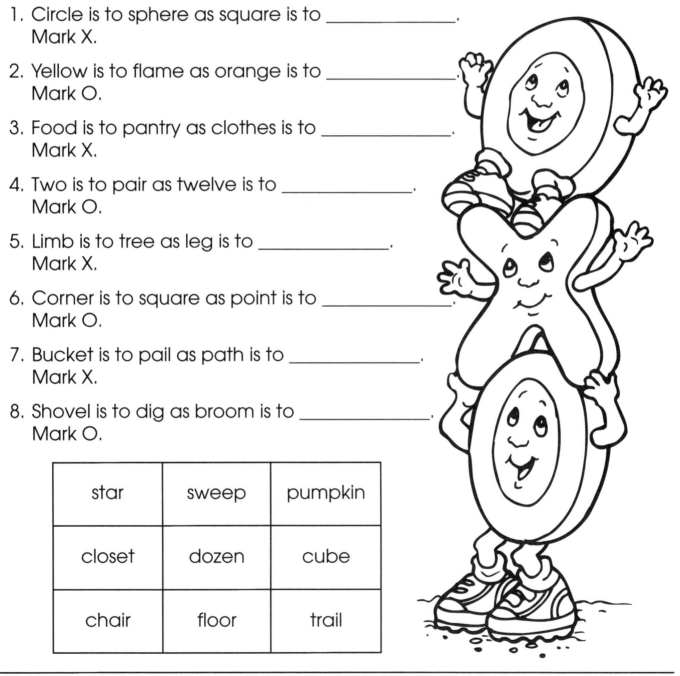

| star | sweep | pumpkin |
|------|-------|---------|
| closet | dozen | cube |
| chair | floor | trail |

Name

## Applying analogies

Unit 8

Remember to look for a relationship between the first set of words, then apply the same relationship to the second set.

Complete each analogy using words from the Word Bank. Then find the answers in the puzzle. They may be written across, down, or diagonally.

1. Wind is to sailboat as oar is to _____.

2. Fly is to frog as mouse is to _____.

3. Sweater is to wool as boot is to _____.

4. Weight is to scale as temperature is to _____.

5. Vase is to flowers as wallet is to _____.

6. Water is to ice as rain is to _____.

7. Carpenter is to hammer as cook is to _____.

8. Scale is to fish as fur is to _____.

9. Paper is to book as glass is to _____.

10. Tractor is to farmer as boat is to _____.

| fisherman | k | r | s | n | o | w | l | d | r | t | l | f |
|-----------|---|---|---|---|---|---|---|---|---|---|---|---|
| thermometer | t | h | e | r | m | o | m | e | t | e | r | i |
| snake | i | b | r | z | n | a | h | c | a | e | k | s |
| money | m | m | g | l | s | t | n | w | p | s | e | h |
| canoe | o | a | u | l | a | h | o | c | a | n | o | e |
| ladle | n | c | m | e | v | d | e | h | w | a | x | r |
| mammal | e | n | l | m | n | m | l | o | i | k | w | m |
| leather | y | f | t | i | a | c | h | e | q | e | f | a |
| window | m | y | w | j | d | l | s | y | a | f | o | n |
| snow | | | | | | | | | | | | |

# Unit 8 Test

### Study Skills, Analogies

Read or listen to the directions. Fill in the circle beside the best answer.

☐ Example:

Which of these would help you find a picture of the flag of Argentina?

(A) card catalog

(B) dictionary

(C) index

(D) encyclopedia

Take time to review your answers.

Answer: D because encyclopedias are books full of factual information.

Now try these. You have 20 minutes. Continue until you see ⬡STOP.

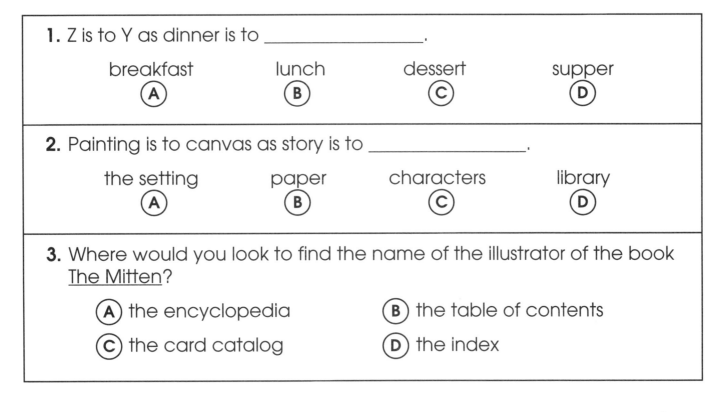

**1.** Z is to Y as dinner is to _____.

breakfast (A)   lunch (B)   dessert (C)   supper (D)

**2.** Painting is to canvas as story is to _____.

the setting (A)   paper (B)   characters (C)   library (D)

**3.** Where would you look to find the name of the illustrator of the book <u>The Mitten</u>?

(A) the encyclopedia   (B) the table of contents

(C) the card catalog   (D) the index

GO ON

Use the bar graph to answer questions 4–6.

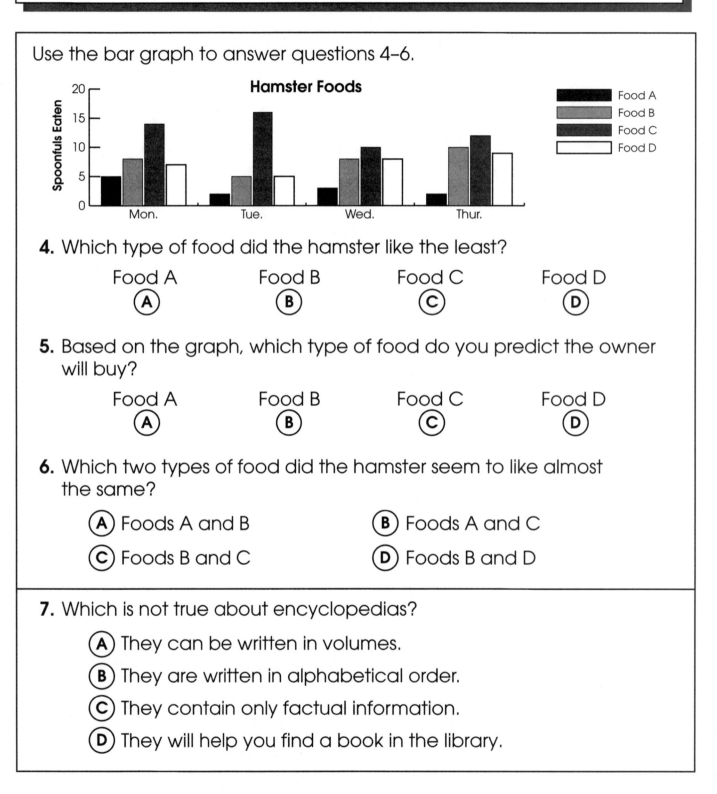

**Hamster Foods**

Spoonfuls Eaten

Legend: Food A, Food B, Food C, Food D

Mon.  Tue.  Wed.  Thur.

**4.** Which type of food did the hamster like the least?

Food A Ⓐ    Food B Ⓑ    Food C Ⓒ    Food D Ⓓ

**5.** Based on the graph, which type of food do you predict the owner will buy?

Food A Ⓐ    Food B Ⓑ    Food C Ⓒ    Food D Ⓓ

**6.** Which two types of food did the hamster seem to like almost the same?

Ⓐ Foods A and B        Ⓑ Foods A and C

Ⓒ Foods B and C        Ⓓ Foods B and D

**7.** Which is not true about encyclopedias?

Ⓐ They can be written in volumes.

Ⓑ They are written in alphabetical order.

Ⓒ They contain only factual information.

Ⓓ They will help you find a book in the library.

GO ON

Use the bar graph to answer questions 8–10.

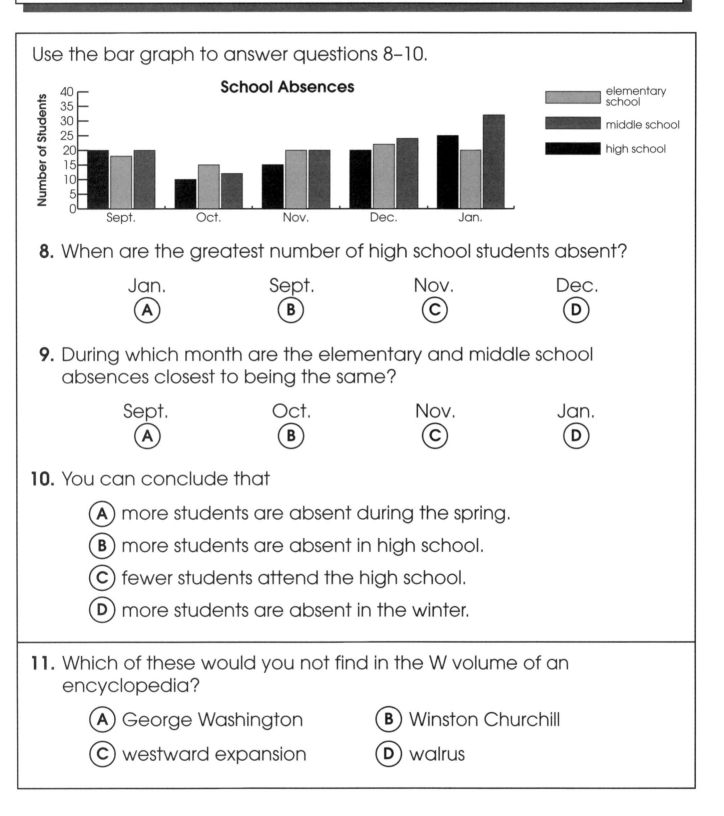

**School Absences**

Number of Students

Sept.  Oct.  Nov.  Dec.  Jan.

elementary school

middle school

high school

**8.** When are the greatest number of high school students absent?

Jan.
Ⓐ

Sept.
Ⓑ

Nov.
Ⓒ

Dec.
Ⓓ

**9.** During which month are the elementary and middle school absences closest to being the same?

Sept.
Ⓐ

Oct.
Ⓑ

Nov.
Ⓒ

Jan.
Ⓓ

**10.** You can conclude that

Ⓐ more students are absent during the spring.

Ⓑ more students are absent in high school.

Ⓒ fewer students attend the high school.

Ⓓ more students are absent in the winter.

**11.** Which of these would you not find in the W volume of an encyclopedia?

Ⓐ George Washington

Ⓑ Winston Churchill

Ⓒ westward expansion

Ⓓ walrus

GO ON

Use the chart to answer questions 12–14.

### Champ the Chimpanzee's Milk Intake

|  | Mon. | Tues. | Wed. | Thurs. | Fri. |
|---|---|---|---|---|---|
| Breakfast | 32 oz. | 36 oz. | 30 oz. | 31 oz. | 29 oz. |
| Lunch | 27 oz. | 26 oz. | 29 oz. | 27 oz. | 34 oz. |
| Dinner | 21 oz. | 24 oz. | 18 oz. | 15 oz. | 17 oz. |

12. From the chart, you can conclude that:

Ⓐ Champ eats more than other chimpanzees.

Ⓑ Champ usually eats more at breakfast.

Ⓒ Champ's most important meal is lunch.

Ⓓ Champ is not offered an afternoon snack.

13. On which two days did Champ eat about the same amount for dinner?

Ⓐ Monday and Tuesday      Ⓑ Tuesday and Thursday

Ⓒ Wednesday and Friday      Ⓓ Monday and Thursday

14. On which day did Champ eat about the same amount for breakfast and lunch?

Mon.        Tues.        Wed.        Thurs.
Ⓐ          Ⓑ            Ⓒ           Ⓓ

15. Hockey is to rink as baseball is to _____.

field        home run        glove        bat
Ⓐ            Ⓑ               Ⓒ           Ⓓ

# Unit 8 Test

Use the graph to answer questions 16–18.

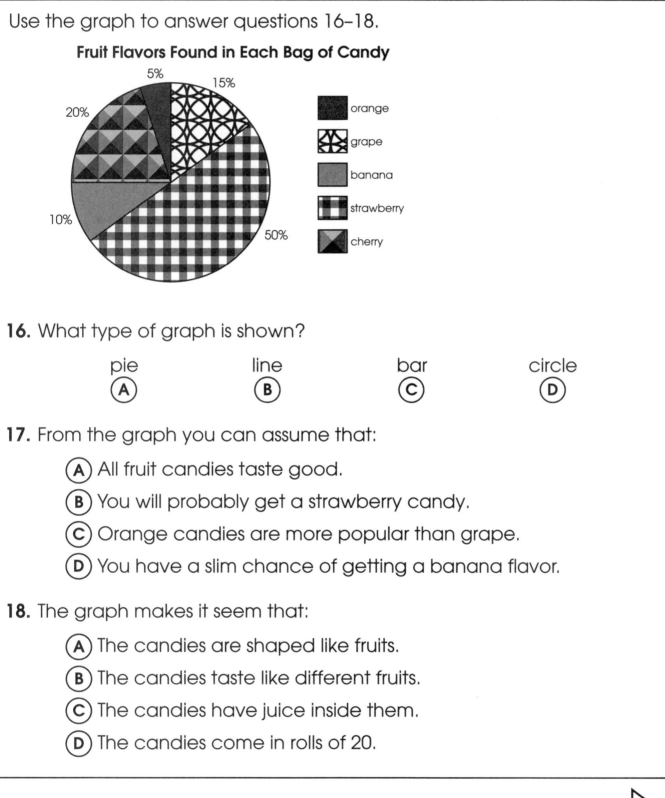

**Fruit Flavors Found in Each Bag of Candy**

- orange
- grape
- banana
- strawberry
- cherry

**16.** What type of graph is shown?

    pie          line          bar          circle

    (A)          (B)          (C)          (D)

**17.** From the graph you can assume that:

(A) All fruit candies taste good.

(B) You will probably get a strawberry candy.

(C) Orange candies are more popular than grape.

(D) You have a slim chance of getting a banana flavor.

**18.** The graph makes it seem that:

(A) The candies are shaped like fruits.

(B) The candies taste like different fruits.

(C) The candies have juice inside them.

(D) The candies come in rolls of 20.

GO ON

**19.** Which of these would help you name the seven wonders of the world?

　Ⓐ encyclopedia　　　　Ⓑ dictionary

　Ⓒ telephone book　　　Ⓓ newspaper

**20.** House is to basement as tree is to _____.

| leaf | nest | wood | roots |
|:---:|:---:|:---:|:---:|
| Ⓐ | Ⓑ | Ⓒ | Ⓓ |

Write an analogy below. Choose two words that are related somehow (color, shape, etc.). Then write two other words that are related in the same way.

_____ is to _____ as

_____ is to _____.

# Final Review Test Name Grid

Write your name in pencil in the boxes along the top. Begin with your last name. Fill in as many letters as will fit. Then follow the columns straight down and bubble in the letters that correspond with the letters in your name. Complete the rest of the information the same way. You may use a piece of scrap paper to help you keep your place.

| STUDENT'S NAME | | SCHOOL |
|---|---|---|
| LAST — FIRST — MI | | TEACHER |

(Name grid: 19 columns of lettered bubbles A–Z for LAST, FIRST, and MI.)

**SCHOOL**

**TEACHER**

FEMALE ○     MALE ○

### DATE OF BIRTH

| MONTH | DAY | YEAR |
|---|---|---|
| JAN ○ | ⓪ ⓪ | ⓪ ⓪ |
| FEB ○ | ① ① | ① ① |
| MAR ○ | ② ② | ② ② |
| APR ○ | ③ ③ | ③ ③ |
| MAY ○ | ④ | ④ ④ |
| JUN ○ | ⑤ | ⑤ ⑤ |
| JUL ○ | ⑥ | ⑥ ⑥ |
| AUG ○ | ⑦ | ⑦ ⑦ |
| SEP ○ | ⑧ | ⑧ ⑧ |
| OCT ○ | ⑨ | ⑨ ⑨ |
| NOV ○ | | |
| DEC ○ | | |

GRADE  ③  ④  ⑤

# Final Review Test Answer Sheet

Pay close attention when transferring your answers. Fill in the bubbles neatly and completely. You may use a piece of scrap paper to help you keep your place.

**SAMPLES**
A Ⓐ Ⓑ ● Ⓓ
B Ⓕ ● Ⓗ Ⓙ

| | | | | |
|---|---|---|---|---|
| 1 Ⓐ Ⓑ Ⓒ Ⓓ | 7 Ⓐ Ⓑ Ⓒ Ⓓ | 13 Ⓐ Ⓑ Ⓒ Ⓓ | 19 Ⓐ Ⓑ Ⓒ Ⓓ | 25 Ⓐ Ⓑ Ⓒ Ⓓ |
| 2 Ⓕ Ⓖ Ⓗ Ⓙ | 8 Ⓕ Ⓖ Ⓗ Ⓙ | 14 Ⓕ Ⓖ Ⓗ Ⓙ | 20 Ⓕ Ⓖ Ⓗ Ⓙ | |
| 3 Ⓐ Ⓑ Ⓒ Ⓓ | 9 Ⓐ Ⓑ Ⓒ Ⓓ | 15 Ⓐ Ⓑ Ⓒ Ⓓ | 21 Ⓐ Ⓑ Ⓒ Ⓓ | |
| 4 Ⓕ Ⓖ Ⓗ Ⓙ | 10 Ⓕ Ⓖ Ⓗ Ⓙ | 16 Ⓕ Ⓖ Ⓗ Ⓙ | 22 Ⓕ Ⓖ Ⓗ Ⓙ | |
| 5 Ⓐ Ⓑ Ⓒ Ⓓ | 11 Ⓐ Ⓑ Ⓒ Ⓓ | 17 Ⓐ Ⓑ Ⓒ Ⓓ | 23 Ⓐ Ⓑ Ⓒ Ⓓ | |
| 6 Ⓕ Ⓖ Ⓗ Ⓙ | 12 Ⓕ Ⓖ Ⓗ Ⓙ | 18 Ⓕ Ⓖ Ⓗ Ⓙ | 24 Ⓕ Ⓖ Ⓗ Ⓙ | |

Read or listen to the directions. Fill in the circle beside the best answer.

❑ Example:
Use the context of the sentence to find the meaning of the underlined word.

Our school day will commence at 9:00.

(A) get busy

(B) turn fun

(C) begin

(D) end

Answer: C because it makes sense that a school day begins at that time.

Now try these. You have 30 minutes.

Continue until you see ⬡STOP .

Remember your Helping Hand Strategies:

1. Reread the paragraphs if you cannot remember an answer.

2. More than one answer may seem correct! Be sure to compare the choices.

3. Use your time wisely. If something seems too tough, skip it and come back later.

4. Take time to review your answers.

5. Transfer your answers carefully. Use a piece of scratch paper to keep your place on the answer sheet.

---

1. Choose the word that has different meanings but makes sense in both sentences.

The _____ led his troops to win the war.
Tony realized that he had made a _____ mistake.

| president | major | big | bad |
|-----------|-------|-----|-----|
| (A) | (B) | (C) | (D) |

---

2. Mark the word that means almost the same as **divide**.

| split | math | multiply | groups |
|-------|------|----------|--------|
| (F) | (G) | (H) | (J) |

GO ON ▷

**3.** Which detail does not follow the main idea?

Fall is such a busy time of year. Not only does school start, but soccer practice and scout meetings begin as well. The trees are always so pretty in the fall.

(A) School starts in the fall.       (B) Soccer practice starts.

(C) Scout meetings begin.       (D) The trees are pretty.

Use the index to answer questions 4 and 5.

| Polar Bears | 43 |
|---|---|
| Poles | |
| North | 28, 30 |
| South | 30–34 |
| Pollution | 67, 78–81 |
| Porpoises | 13, 17 |

**4.** Which page will not help you learn about pollution?

page 67       page 79       page 80       page 77
(F)            (G)            (H)            (J)

**5.** What will you learn about on page 32?

polar bears       North Pole       South Pole       pollution
(A)                (B)              (C)              (D)

**6.** Mark the sentence that is a fact.

(F) The ferris wheel is the dullest ride at the carnival.

(G) The carnival runs from Wednesday to Sunday.

(H) Saturday is the best day to go.

(J) The "Cat Screech" is the most exciting ride.

GO ON ➤

# Final Review Test

Read the story to answer questions 7–10.

## Our Family Tree

The old oak tree was over 60 years old. It had been standing in its place long before my mother was born. My grandmother remembered the day her father planted the tree. He knew that the tree would become part of the family.

He was right. My grandmother and grandfather got married under the tree. Years later, my mother climbed the tree to play hide-and-seek. Just last year, my dad and I built a great fort among the tree's strong branches.

This year we will plan a party for the tree's 65th birthday. We are planning to hang balloons from its branches and twirl garland around its trunk. Our family will enjoy our last picnic of the summer in the tree's shade and eat slices of birthday cake. It will be just like any other family member's celebration!

**7.** How old is the tree?

60  
Ⓐ

65  
Ⓑ

70  
Ⓒ

75  
Ⓓ

**8.** Who planted the tree?

Ⓕ the author

Ⓖ the author's grandmother

Ⓗ the author's dad

Ⓙ the author's great-grandfather

**9.** Why is the family planning a party?

Ⓐ The family wants to have a picnic.

Ⓑ The tree is having a birthday.

Ⓒ The author's mother is having a birthday.

Ⓓ To celebrate the end of summer.

**GO ON**

**10.** How is the tree not like a family member?

(F) It lives with the family.

(G) It shares in the family's fun.

(H) It makes the family feel good.

(J) It likes to eat birthday cake.

**11.** Which of these can you conclude from the sentence?

Joseph's mom watched with astonishment as her son ate every bite of meat loaf, spinach noodles, and asparagus.

(A) Joseph is in fourth grade.

(B) Joseph does not usually eat these foods.

(C) Joseph's mom was serving his favorite dessert.

(D) Joseph was hungry.

Read the paragraph to answer questions 12 and 13.

Tia skipped all the way home from the bus stop. She had missed her new puppy while she was at school. She ran into the laundry room to find him, tripping over one of her new shoes on the floor. As she turned the corner, she noticed her favorite shirt thrown on the ground. Then Tia let out a scream.

**12.** What do you think Tia saw?

(F) torn clothes scattered about

(G) her puppy in the washing machine

(H) another new puppy

(J) her mom doing laundry

# Final Review Test

**13.** Which of these would probably not be found in the laundry room?

baskets
(A)

hangers
(B)

soap
(C)

pill box
(D)

Read the story to answer questions 14–18.

## Double Trouble

Stephen and Michael are not only best friends, they are twin brothers. Though they look exactly alike, it is easy to tell them apart by their actions. If you run into one of them at the library or the music store, you know it is Stephen. If you see one of them practicing soccer goals or skating, it is Michael. But it has not always been that way.

When the boys were in kindergarten, Stephen thought the older kids would like him more if he was a good athlete. He tried to keep up with his brother, but it was difficult for him. Soon he became known as the "slow one." Stephen felt lonely for the first time in his life. His brother had new friends, and he had none.

When Michael noticed how sad Stephen was, the boys developed a plan. The next day at school, the boys traded shirts in the bathroom just before recess. Stephen, dressed as Michael, told his friends his ankle was hurt, and he would not be able to play at recess. Then the real Michael, wearing Stephen's shirt, played soccer with the other kids. At the end of recess, the other kids apologized to "Stephen" for calling him names. The plan worked perfectly, but Stephen was still singing the blues. He knew that he would have to find something he was really good at.

Then one day at school, Ms. Green asked Stephen if he would represent their class in the school reading contest. Stephen had always loved to read so he agreed. Ever since Stephen won the competition, he has always been happy doing the things he loves best.

**14.** From this story, you can tell that:

- (F) Michael is too busy to help his brother.
- (G) Michael's new friends are important to him.
- (H) Michael wants his brother to be happy.
- (J) Michael will be on the football team.

**15.** How are the brothers alike?

- (A) They both love to read.
- (B) They both love to play sports.
- (C) They both love music.
- (D) They both care about each other.

**16.** Which of these was a solution to Stephen's problem?

- (F) Michael pretended to be Stephen.
- (G) Michael stopped playing soccer.
- (H) Stephen found something he was good at doing.
- (J) Stephen quit playing sports.

**17.** How do you think Stephen acts at recess now?

- (A) He probably plays other games.
- (B) He probably will not play at all.
- (C) He may feel sorry for himself.
- (D) He may stay home from school.

GO ON

**18.** What does it mean to be "singing the blues"?

    (F) to be a good singer    (G) to be unhappy

    (H) to be colorful    (J) to be cheerful

Use the graph to answer questions 19–21.

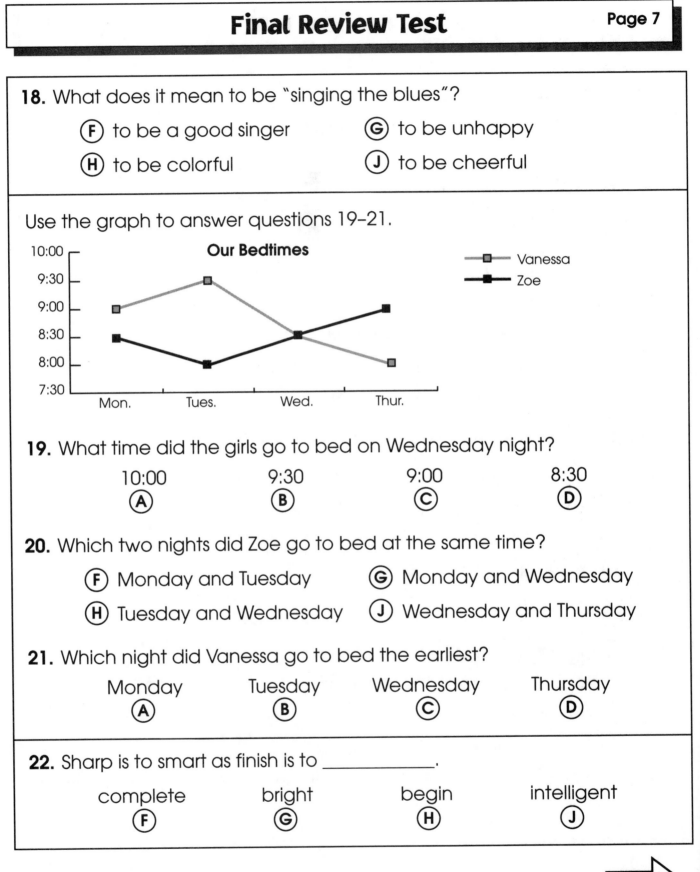

**Our Bedtimes**

■ Vanessa
■ Zoe

**19.** What time did the girls go to bed on Wednesday night?

    10:00      9:30      9:00      8:30

    (A)      (B)      (C)      (D)

**20.** Which two nights did Zoe go to bed at the same time?

    (F) Monday and Tuesday    (G) Monday and Wednesday

    (H) Tuesday and Wednesday    (J) Wednesday and Thursday

**21.** Which night did Vanessa go to bed the earliest?

    Monday    Tuesday    Wednesday    Thursday

    (A)      (B)      (C)      (D)

**22.** Sharp is to smart as finish is to _____.

    complete    bright    begin    intelligent

    (F)      (G)      (H)      (J)

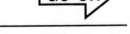

GO ON

**23.** Mark the drawing of the student who followed the directions.

Draw a white rectangle next to a black circle with a striped triangle in it.

Ⓐ     Ⓑ     Ⓒ     Ⓓ

**24.** Which of these would you not find in the P volume of an encyclopedia?

pyrite     president     Pete Rose     Wiley Post
Ⓕ     Ⓖ     Ⓗ     Ⓙ

**25.** Which word does not belong in the group?

lungs     brain     legs     heart
Ⓐ     Ⓑ     Ⓒ     Ⓓ

Write the title of a story you know well. Then write a sentence telling the story's main idea.

TITLE: _____

MAIN IDEA: _____

_____

# Answer Key

## Page 5

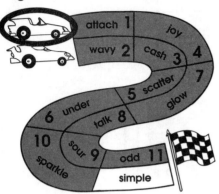

## Page 6

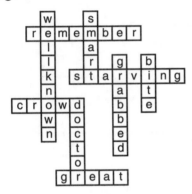

## Page 7

A POSTAGE STAMP!

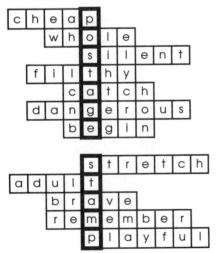

## Page 8

1. E; 2. F; 3. B; 4. G; 5. A; 6. C; 7. D

## Page 9

1. break; 2. book; 3. mean; 4. tire;
5. land; 6. free; 7. glasses; 8. straw

## Page 10

Answers will vary.

## Page 11

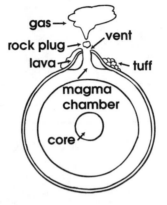

## Page 12

1. told not to; 2. sweater; 3. drops of water; 4. rest; 5. working together;
6. special; 7. popped; 8. homes;
9. sharp hairs

## Unit 1 Test

1. B; 2. D; 3. C; 4. A; 5. C; 6. D;
7. A; 8. B; 9. D; 10. B; 11. C; 12. D;
13. A; 14. B; 15. C; 16. D; 17. D;
18. C; 19. B; 20. A; Constructed-response answers will vary.

## Page 18

Check students' pages.

## Page 19

1. 4, 51; 2. 7, 90; 3. 1, 3; 4. 5, 64;
5. 2, 25; 6. 3, 39; 7. 6, 72; 8. 1, 3;
9. 7, 90; 10. 5, 64

## Page 20

1. 1, 3, 2, 5, 4; 2. 2, 3, 1, 5, 4; 3. 5, 4, 2, 3, 1; 4. 1, 4, 3, 5, 2; 5. 3, 4, 5, 1, 2; 6. 1, 5, 4, 2, 3

## Page 21

1. page 92; 2. page 56; 3. shingle;
4. page 76; 5. children; 6. horses

## Page 22

1. 2; 2. cuter, cutest; 3. noun;
4. 3; 5. adjective; 6. having little or no light

## Page 23

cowl; curd; curlew; curlicue; currant; currency; curvet; cusk; cyan

## Page 24

1. lamp; 2. learn; 3. large; 4. lane;
5. locket; 6. lobster; 7. listen;
8. lion; 9. low; 10. loud; 11. lot;
12. love

## Unit 2 Test

1. C; 2. D; 3. A; 4. A; 5. D; 6. B; 7. D;
8. A; 9. C; 10. B; 11. D; 12. C; 13. A;
14. B; 15. A; 16. C; 17. D; 18. A;
19. A; 20. D; Constructed-response answers will vary.

## Page 30

1. math book; 2. at the golf course;
3. within an hour of their 2:00 time;
4. goalie; 5. Jonathan's sister;
6. 4:30; 7. Will; 8. late

## Page 31

## Pages 32–33

1. What Is the Dead Sea?; 2. The Salty Waters of the Dead Sea;
3. The Uses of the Dead Sea;
4. The Water Cycle of the Dead Sea

## Page 34

1. C; 2. C; 3. B

# Answer Key

## Page 35

1. TS = Some people like the fire department across the street from our neighborhood, and some people do not.; SD = My mom and dad think it is great because they know that help could reach us within minutes. Nan's parents do not like it because of all the noise the sirens make.; 2. TS = Every evening, Gabriel and his dad look forward to feeding the deer in their backyard.; SD (any two of the following) = Gabriel carries the dried corn from the garage to the edge of the woods. He and his dad spread the corn, then hide behind the edge of the house to watch. Each evening, the same four female deer come to feed.; 3. TS = Alley worked hard to finish all of her projects at summer camp.; SD (any two of the following) = She tie-dyed her shirt in shades of blue and purple, glued eyes onto her lion's mask, carefully formed a monkey out of clay.

## Page 36

TS = Pike's Peak is the name given to one of the mountains located in the Rocky Mountains of Colorado.; TS = The Royal Gorge is a deep canyon that was created by the snow and rain that run off the Rocky Mountains and into rivers.; Supporting details will vary.

## Unit 3 Test

1. C; 2. A; 3. B; 4. D; 5. A; 6. C; 7. B; 8. A; 9. D; 10. B; 11. D; 12. D; 13. B; 14. A; 15. D; 16. C; 17. B; 18. C; 19. A; 20. D; Constructed response: 30, 20, 40, 50, 10

## Page 44

1. Birds of Prey; 2. after; 3. Wildcat Wackiness and Penguins on Parade; 4. The Reptile Review; 5. The Monkey Movie; 6. Penguin Palace

## Page 45

1. 1st, Before, 2nd, Now; 2. 2nd, soon, 1st, immediately; 3.1st, First, 2nd, Next; 4. 1st, earlier, 2nd, finally ; 5. 1st, right away, 2nd, eventually; 6. 2nd, someday, 1st, soon; 7. 1st, eventually, 2nd, never; 8. 2nd, later, 1st, immediately

## Page 46

4, 2, 3, 6, 1, 5

## Page 47

1. C; 2. D; 3. A; 4. B

## Page 48

1. He was giving them to Pete.; 2. He could not buy any more until hid dad got paid.; 3. His pencil was completely used up, and the eraser was totally gone.; 4. Timothy had helped Pete.

## Unit 4 Test

1. D; 2. A; 3. C; 4. C; 5. B; 6. A; 7. B; 8. C; 9. B; 10. A; 11. B; 12. D; 13. A; 14. B; 15. A; 16. D; 17. C; 18. D;  19. C; 20. D; Constructed-response answers will vary.

## Midway Review Test

1. C; 2. J; 3. B; 4. F; 5. C; 6. G; 7. D; 8. J; 9. B; 10. F; 11. C; 12. F; 13. D; 14. H; 15. A; 16. F; 17. C; 18. G; 19. D; 20. J; Constructed-response answers will vary.

## Page 65

Answers will vary.

## Page 66

Answers will vary.

## Page 67

1. a; 2. b, c; 3. c, d

## Page 68

1. no; 2. yes; 3. yes; 4. no; 5. yes; 6. no; 7. no

## Page 69

Answers will vary. Possible answers include: 1. they help you, one uses nails; 2. they hold clothes, one can be carried; 3. they can be found in a house, one is living; 4. you can learn something from them, one is made of paper

## Page 70

Answers will vary. Possible answers include: Alike: 1. they both use gas., 2. they are a great way to get around., 3. they are both available as convertibles.; Different: 1. old cars could not go very fast., 2. in old cars, the gas tank was under the front seat., 3. some old cars did not have bumpers or mirrors.

## Unit 5 Test

1. D; 2. D; 3. A; 4. B; 5. A; 6. C; 7. A; 8. B; 9. D; 10. C; 11. B; 12. D; 13. A; 14. C; 15. D; 16. C; 17. B; 18. C; 19. A; 20. B; Constructed-response answers will vary.

## Page 79

1. Fact; 2. Opinion; 3. Opinion; 4. Fact; 5. Opinion; 6. Fact; 7. Fact; 8. Opinion; 9. Opinion; 10. Opinion; 11. Fact; 12. Opinion; 13. Fact; 14.–17. Answers will vary.

## Page 80

Answers will vary. Possible answers include: Facts: 1. Native Americans use dance to express themselves., 2. Each dance has emotional meaning., 3. The Great Plains tribes do the Fancy Dance.; Opinions: 1. The Fancy Dance is the most exciting dance.; 2. The Hoop Dance is the most difficult dance.; 3. The Butterfly Dance is beautiful.

# Answer Key

## Page 81

1789–1799: 1. G. Washington,
2. J. Adams; 1800–1849:
1. T. Jefferson, 2. J. Monroe,
3. M. Van Buren, 4. J. Polk;
1850–1899: 1. A. Lincoln,
2. U. Grant, 3. G. Cleveland;
1900–1949: 1. T. Roosevelt,
2. W. Wilson, 3. H. Hoover,
4. H. Truman; 1950–1999:
1. J. Kennedy, 2. G. Ford,
3. R. Reagan, 4. B. Clinton;
2000–2001: G. W. Bush

## Page 82

1. sock; 2. Uranus; 3. paper clip;
4. apple; 5. dolphin; 6. pink;
7. mirror; 8. heart; 9. eyebrows;
10. vacuum; 11. window; 12. Ben Franklin

## Page 83

1. Mickey dropped the bowl.;
2. sitting in a pile of dust.; 3. Mickey and Jonathan ran toward the big bag of dog food.; 4. "I think you've already helped enough today."

## Page 84

Answers will vary. Possible answers include: 1. The dog will join the donkey.; 2. because they share the same problem; 3. Go inside to eat.; 4. The robbers were going. Also, there was a table full of food, and they were hungry.; 5. They will live in the house.

## Unit 6 Test

1. B; 2. A; 3. C; 4. D; 5. D; 6. A;
7. C; 8. B; 9. A; 10. B; 11. C; 12. D;
13. C; 14. A; 15. A; 16. C; 17. A;
18. C; 19. B; 20. A; Constructed-response answers will vary.

## Page 91

Answers will vary. Possible answers include: 1. polite, excited;
2. stubborn, selfish; 3. sorry, fair

## Page 92

Answers will vary. Possible answers include:1. He was lonely.; 2. He made a new friend.; 3. His new friend could not play inside.;
4. He played outside instead.

## Page 93

Check students' drawings.

## Pages 94–95

Answers will vary.

## Page 96

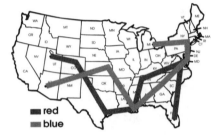

■ red
■ blue

## Unit 7 Test

1. D; 2. C; 3. A; 4. B; 5. C; 6. B;
7. A; 8. D; 9. A; 10. D; 11. B; 12. C;
13. B; 14. B; 15. A; 16. C; 17. D;
18. A; 19. D; 20. C; Constructed-response answers will vary.

## Page 104

1. 15; 2. 16; 3. 1; 4. 16; 5. 9; 6. 1;
7. 21; 8. 19

## Page 105

Answers will vary.

## Page 106

1. E; 2. C; 3. A; 4. B; 5. D; 6. B

## Page 107

1. record; 2. edit; 3. Thursday;
4. math; 5. nothing; 6. Tuesday;
7. Friday; 8. rough draft

## Page 108

1. February; 2. April; 3. snow;
4. January and February; 5. April and May

## Page 109

1. cube; 2. pumpkin; 3. closet;
4. dozen; 5. chair; 6. star; 7. trail;
8. sweep

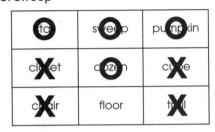

## Page 110

1. canoe; 2. snake; 3. leather;
4. thermometer; 5. money; 6. snow;
7. ladle; 8. mammal; 9. window;
10. fisherman

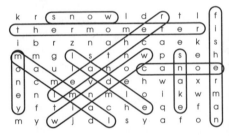

## Unit 8 Test

1. B; 2. B; 3. C; 4. A; 5. C; 6. D; 7. D;
8. A; 9. C; 10. D; 11. B; 12. B; 13. C;
14. C; 15. A; 16. A; 17. B; 18. B;
19. A; 20. D; Constructed-response answers will vary.

## Final Review Test

1. B; 2. F; 3. D; 4. J; 5. C; 6. G; 7. B;
8. J; 9. B; 10. J; 11. B; 12. F; 13. D;
14. H; 15. D; 16. H; 17. A; 18. G;
19. D; 20. G; 21. D; 22. F; 23. A;
24. H; 25. C; Constructed-response answers will vary.